HAMLET

AND THE DISTRACTED GLOBE

TEXT AND CONTEXT

Editors

ARNOLD KETTLE
Professor of Literature, Open University

and

A. K. THORLBY
Professor of Comparative Literature
University of Sussex

*

MICHAEL EGAN
Mark Twain's Huckleberry Finn:
Race, Class and Society

ANDREW GURR
Hamlet and the Distracted Globe

BERNARD HARRISON
Henry Fielding's Tom Jones:
The Novelist as Moral Philosopher

JEREMY HAWTHORN
Virginia Woolf's Mrs. Dalloway:
A Study in Alienation

DOUGLAS JEFFERSON
Jane Austen's Emma:
A Landmark in English Fiction

LAURENCE LERNER
Thomas Hardy's The Mayor of Casterbridge:
Tragedy or Social History?

A. D. NUTTALL
Dostoevsky's Crime and Punishment

PETER WIDDOWSON
E. M. Forster's Howards End

Other Titles in Preparation

HAMLET

and the distracted globe

Andrew Gurr

*Professor of English Literature
in the University of Reading*

SUSSEX UNIVERSITY PRESS

1978

Published for
SUSSEX UNIVERSITY PRESS

by

SCOTTISH ACADEMIC PRESS
33 Montgomery Street
Edinburgh EH7 5JX

*

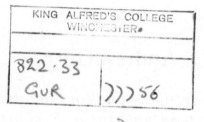
Hardback ISBN 85621 069 2
Paperback ISBN 85621 070 6
©Andrew Gurr 1978

Printed Offset Litho in Great Britain by
Sussex University Printing Unit

To
SAINT PATRICK

CONTENTS

1. Organisation and Structure		*Page*	9
2. The Claudian Globe			26
3. Hamlet's Globe (1): Blood and Judgement			42
4. Hamlet's Globe (2): Scourge and Minister			62
5. The Sequence of Events			80
Notes			115

Chapter 1

ORGANISATION AND STRUCTURE

Hamlet's head, he tells us, is a "distracted globe". Alert like his creator to every nuance of situation and language, he captures in a single pun all three of the central features of the play. His metaphor is taken from the story of Hercules, the archetypal man of action, who took on his shoulders the burden of the heavens, the celestial globe carried by Atlas. The burden on Hamlet's shoulders is his own head, a globe more lunatic than heavenly, distracted from its proper function by the discovery that his uncle has murdered his father the king. To Elizabethans a man's head was the "heavenly" part of him, containing God's twin gifts of speech and reason, the qualities which raise man above the beasts. Fratricide and regicide, the murder of a king by his brother, were such ungodly acts as to "distract" any man's head from its proper functions of honest speech and moral reasoning.

But when Hamlet speaks of "*this* distracted globe", and clutches his head with the pain of it, his thought is not only self-centred. The sphere he inhabits, the earthly globe, must be lunatic too if such things can happen in it. The world is not the moral and rational place that it should be. Claudius the murderer, and all the apparatus of the obedient court which surrounds and supports him, represent a world which has turned its proper values upside down. At the end of the play, when Hamlet ostensibly apologises to Laertes for the lunatic slaughter of his father Polonius, he obliquely accuses Claudius of madness. Crime is a form of insanity, since to destroy goodness and distract the world from its moral courses calls for an inversion of true reason. To invert moral values is ultimately insane, says Hamlet.

Hamlet's is a double metaphor, of distraction in the world at large and a distraction in his head mirroring the larger disorder. This is the situation from which the play's action

9

develops. But besides that double significance his pun had still another layer of meaning for his own times. Elizabethan actors liked to think of themselves as presenting a picture of the world in miniature on their stages. Shakespeare's own acting company used the idea when they named their theatre, built a year before *Hamlet* was written, the "Globe". Its motto was *totus mundus agit histrionem*, roughly translatable as all the world's a stage. The flag with which they signalled their performances was a figure of Hercules shouldering the globe.[1] Rosencrantz's reference to "Hercules and his load" (II.ii.345) is an allusion to the theatre in which the play was first staged. So Hamlet's pun also alluded directly to his first audiences. And more than that, it applies to all audiences who have seen the play since, as all the other uses of the "play" metaphor in *Hamlet* will confirm. The audiences which packed the Globe in 1600 came for the "distraction" of Shakespeare's play in a deeper sense than they necessarily knew. They came for entertainment, distraction from more serious matters. And they will have reason not to forget this entertainment quickly. "Remember thee!" says Hamlet to his dead father,

> Ay, thou poor ghost, while memory holds a seat
> In this distracted globe.

$$(I.v.95-7)[2]$$

Hamlet's story may be a "play", a game, and the "action" of his revenge may be "acting" only in the theatrical sense, but the hint is there in his pun that these are serious matters we are viewing in our search for distraction. When at the end of the play Hamlet urges Horatio to "tell my story" in "this harsh world" it is no ordinary fiction he wants broadcast. The play is an image of human morality, and as such it demands serious attention.

In those three varieties of distraction – Hamlet's anguish, Denmark's moral lunacy and the audience's desire for a "play" about something serious – lies the triple subject of *Hamlet*. The play presents us with a compellingly graphic diagram of the conflict between morality and expediency in the guise of an entertainment.

10

In essence the play exhibits the conflict between Hamlet's inner world, his acute sense of a moral universe governing human conduct, and the outside world of Claudius's government. Claudius's is the world of appearances, of polite seeming which can smile and smile and be villainous. Claudius is the man who puts his ambition before moral government, the proper use of the divine gift of reason. Hamlet is the man who sees through all the pretences, the "seeming" and "acting", so that his mind mirrors in anguish all the monstrous imperfections of the globe around him. Added to that anguish is the knowledge that because he alone sees the imperfections for what they are he alone can act to correct them. And by doing so he will inevitably be drawn into that imperfect globe. In an imperfect world the only means to correct imperfections are themselves imperfect. Hamlet has to do evil to correct evil. In that way his distraction is a true mirror of the madness of the Claudian world.

The context for *Hamlet* therefore, seen from a modern perspective, is the ageless debate over whether ends justify means. The absolute morality of a Hamlet, faced with the expedient ruthlessness of a Claudius, makes him choose between ruthless action of the kind Claudius excels in and suffering in private. His choice will depend on his decision whether the end of destroying Claudius can justify the means he must adopt if he is to succeed. He could suffer under this monstrous hypocrite or he could commit murder. No other course was really open to him.

In this small capsule Shakespeare fitted the whole political question that lay at the heart of sixteenth-century thinking about monarchies. When authority to govern is in the hands of one man, and he has that authority for the whole of his natural life, practical restraints on his use of that authority are difficult to maintain. The law gets its authority from him, so the law can't be used against him without losing that authority. More practically, since he controls law enforcement, who is to enforce it against him if he should choose to break it? Political commentators since Aristotle had made a distinction between kings, those rulers who observed the law, and tyrants,

11

who broke it. No commentator however had a readily acceptable answer to the question how to deal with tyrants. In the sixteenth century Catholics said the Pope had authority over unlawful kings. Calvin said the "lesser magistrates" could depose them. In England Parliament was always used to ratify a new ruler since it represented the country in the social contract between ruler and ruled, but Parliament was not yet in a position to proclaim its authority as an alternative to the king's. In the end there was no court of appeal against tyranny except God, whose verdict was usually inscrutable. La Fontaine's fable about belling the cat, the problem of which mouse should take responsibility for fastening a bell round its neck, is a wry comment on the question.

Despite this difficulty there were writers, especially the Huguenot monarchomachs, who held that rebellion against an unjust king, and even assassination, might sometimes be justifiable. The Scotsman George Buchanan, once tutor to the infant James I, went so far as to claim that

God, angered at the people, sends tyrants ... who punish those who deserve to be punished ... but it is equally true that God has called poor and almost unknown men from the ranks of the common people to execute vengeance on an arrogant and worthless tyrant.[3]

James himself of course took the opposite view, or rather the first half of Buchanan's view. Tyrants were God's infliction on a sinful people, and therefore must be suffered in patience. The only legitimate action was to offer "sobbes and teares to God" for the tyrant's amendment.

The question of justifiable regicide, tyrannicide, was the most acute form of the sixteenth-century version of the ends-justifying-means debate. Assassination was the most practicable form of political action in states where monarchs ruled for life and where there was no legal machinery to depose them. It was the kind of action associated with the ruthlessness of Machiavelli's Italy, but it was widely practised nonetheless. The Papal Bull *De visibili monarchia* of 1570 which excommunicated Elizabeth of England was freely interpreted as an invitation to assassinate her, since it released Catholics from the obligation of obedience to a heretical prince.

To this theoretical and practical question, what circumstances might justify an individual taking the law into his own hands and committing regicide, Shakespeare applied *Hamlet*. He picked up the popular blood and thunder tradition of the revenge play and gave it a moral resonance by putting the emphasis not on the blood but on the individual's quandary between tyrannicide and the alternative virtue of Christian suffering, leaving vengeance to God.

The revenge play formula trims the question down to its bare essentials. Instead of a general tyranny, one subject alone has a specific grievance against his king. Since the grievance is against the king he can get no redress by course of law. The individual then has to weigh his own advantage in getting redress for his grievances and helping the general good by removing a tyrant against his own loss of virtue in spilling blood and the general disorder that follows regicide. Leaving vengeance to God, as God enjoins, and suffering virtuously is always there as an alternative. Does, then, the end of destroying tyranny justify the criminal means?

Hamlet was the first revenge drama to take the moral question into account, though essayists had long found it a popular subject. Such possible influences on Shakespeare's thinking about it as we can find are all in the essayists, not the playwrights of his time. He did not think in narrowly literary traditions. In fact the one work that shows clear signs of having influenced Shakespeare's thinking is Montaigne's essay *Of Profit and Honesty*. It was translated from the original French by Florio, a man known to Shakespeare, in about 1599, and published in 1603. Shakespeare evidently read the translation before its publication, because distinctive words and phrases of Florio's are peppered throughout *Hamlet*'s text. In his essay Montaigne muses on the question how far personal honesty might be compromised in the interests of political expediency. How far should public profit, patriotism, justify personal dishonesty?

Montaigne's evidence is largely a collection of historical

practical
rather
than moral

13

incidents, cases of immoral actions done out of patriotism or a concern for justice. Some of his anecdotes have a direct bearing on Hamlet's case. At one end of the problem, says Montaigne,

> It is reported, that *Witoldus* Prince of *Lituania*, introduced an order with that nation, which was that the partie condemned to die, should with his owne hands make himselfe away; finding it strange, that a third man being guiltlesse of the fact, should be employed and charged to commit a murther.[4]

Hamlet is unique among Shakespeare's tragic heroes in being totally innocent himself of any crime when the play's action begins. He is called on to execute Claudius for his crime through no more complicity than being a blood relation of the victim of the crime.

A more direct illustration of the problem for Montaigne is the case of Timoleon, who "with a brotherlie hand . . . slew the tyrant". That was a truly painful decision, says Montaigne. "And it neerelie pinched his self-gnawne conscience, that he was compelled to purchase the common good, at the rate of his honestie." Opinion on his decision was divided.

> The sacred Senate it selfe, by his means delivered
> from thraldome, durst not definitivelie decide of
> so haughty an action, and rend in two so urgent and
> different semblances.

The question of judging his conduct was ingeniously settled by the Syracusans, who made him their governor, and set as the test of his virtue his subsequent handling of the rod of justice:

> that according as he should well or ill demeane
> himselfe in his charge, their sentence should encline,
> either to grace him as the redeemer of his country,
> or disgrace him, as the murtherer of his brother.[5]

Under such a constraint Timoleon of course acted well, and Montaigne concludes "this mans end is excusable, if ever any could be".

But Timoleon is not Montaigne's ultimate model. After describing his last noble example, Epaminondas, Montaigne finally comes to the conclusion that personal honesty is a greater consideration than public expediency.

> Let us not feare, after so great a maister, to
> hold that some things are unlawfull, even against
> our fellest enemies: that publike interest ought
> not to chalenge all of all, against private interest.[6]

And he ends, quoting a bloodthirsty revenge speech from the Latin writer Lucan (faintly echoed in *Hamlet* at II.ii.454 and elsewhere),

> I abhorre the enraged admonitions of this other unrulie spirite.
> > While swords are brandisht, let no show of grace
> > Once moove you, nor your parents face to face,
> > But with your swords disturbe their reverend grace.
> Let us bereave wicked, bloodie and trayterous dispositions of this pretext of reason: leave we that impious and ex- orbitant justice, and adhere unto more humane imitations.

Revenge, says Montaigne, is an "impious and exorbitant" form of earthly justice. Humanity, grace of soul, is more important.

Whether Shakespeare took much of his colouring for *Hamlet* from Montaigne except in the occasional vivid phrase or word we do not know. By far the longest echo is Polonius's comically ponderous advice to Laertes in I.iii, surely a parody if an echo at all. To see *Hamlet* as simply reflecting Montaigne's thoughts is to underrate it grotesquely. Shakespeare did infinitely more than inject Montaigne's moral calculations over regicide into revenge drama. He humanised the question by displaying the pressures the whole problem of choice lays on Hamlet. It is the human considerations Shakespeare brings into account in the process of dramatising Montaigne's thoughts which make *Hamlet* the stupendous achievement it is.

Montaigne's view of the individual's dilemma over moral questions in politics begs a multitude of questions, because it leaves altogether out of account the complexities of the human

15

psyche. To Montaigne the moral choice may be obscure, but the faculty of human reason which sets out the choice is not. The good man, he assumes, is a perfectly rational, dispassionate creature wholly capable of making his decision on moral grounds alone. A man's rational judgement, the moral part of him, should completely rule the urgings of his blood. To Elizabethans the blood was the great stimulant of human passions, the non-rational "will" or animal part of man, constantly struggling against the head, the divine part, for control of human conduct. Revenge drama was sometimes called the "tragedy of blood". For Montaigne man was only a moral and rational being when his judgement ruled his blood and the animal part of him was held down. Shakespeare saw man as less easily perfectible than that. Hamlet speaks of man's "godlike reason" as the quality which raises him above mere beasts, but when he looks for words to praise the loyal and honest Horatio he calls him a man in whom "blood and judgement are so well commingled", not a slave to his passion but not devoid of it either. Shakespeare's morality is more human than Montaigne's.

The human dimension which Shakespeare adds to Montaigne's consideration of the moral problem of ends and means sets the critic his main challenge: to trace the shape of Hamlet's whole mentality as he confronts his problem and evolves his solution. The moral component is there in Hamlet's thinking. He is continually aware of man's moral "capability and godlike reason" and in how beastlike a way the inhabitants of the Claudian world misuse it. But swamping that consciousness are the tides of his own blood and the passion of his response to Claudius's crime, a passion he can see no ready means of translating into moral action. Moral uncertainty is a mental process not easily separable from emotional incapacity. His moral consciousness is implicit in his reference to the "distracted", irrational globe; in his concern for man's honesty; in his eventual and reluctant acceptance of his role as "scourge and minister", God's instrument to punish the tyrant; and in many other oblique allusions to the moral aspect of his task as revenger. But the considerations that Montaigne weighs so

16

judiciously are insignificant beside the pressures of Hamlet's blood. This is why he spends so little time considering the purely moral aspect of his problem. Only Claudius in the play makes anything of the difficulties inherent in killing monarchs ("There's such divinity doth hedge a king"). And since Claudius is a regicide himself that claim has more effrontery than force in it.

Hamlet seems determined to retain his problem as a personal one, and not to make it a political question of removing a tyrant. He emphasises his own revenge rather than earthly justice. His criterion is "conscience", not Montaigne's "publike commoditie". Only in a negative sense, in keeping his filthy task to himself and not letting anyone else be contaminated with it, does the moral element seem to weigh heavily with him. The feeling of resignation with which he finally faces his task is a submission to the need to commit the crime of murder, but unlike Laertes, also a revenger, who calls on the mob to help with his task, Hamlet will not let others share in the bloodshed.

This reluctance of Hamlet's to admit any weight in the moral component of his task leaves a hole in the play where it matters most. By that I mean it is crucially important that the hole should be there. Neither Hamlet nor Shakespeare is willing to spell out the items which carry weight in Hamlet's mental conflict. Hamlet is tightlipped on the question where our curiosity is sharpest. In his soliloquies he displays his state of mind but not all its contents. And his silence is the chief cause of the flood of speculation over what really was the shape of his mental conflict. Hamlet's mind is a black hole at the centre of the play, and the essence of the play's quality as a picture of the way a man faces appalling obligations. Tracing the hole's outline is our main task.

Montaigne and the other Christian and classical writers[7] who helped to put together a vision of man as a moral being are not necessarily relevant to *Hamlet* as we read it today. They only help to alert us to some of the underlying components in Hamlet's mind. They illustrate one form of the perennial debate over ends and means. Other views in different

17

contexts probably have an equal value in helping to put Hamlet's situation in perspective. I find an affinity, for instance, in Hamlet's eventual acceptance of the solitary role of "scourge and minister" with Wole Soyinka's declaration that "a man dies every time there is silence in the face of tyranny". Suffering in silence is not every man's idea of a moral choice. Hamlet's refusal to bow under the Claudian regime of seeming and dissembling, and especially his insistence that his "story" be proclaimed once his "conscience" has led him to destroy Claudius, is a victory for reason and honesty over bestiality and hypocrisy. There are more considerations under heaven and earth than are dreamed of in Montaigne's philosophy.

Soyinka's preference of moral conduct in politics is the opposite choice to Montaigne's. Neither preference is really directly applicable to Hamlet's conduct of his revenge — certainly neither can be deployed as any sort of basis for evaluating his actions. What they do offer is parallel acknowledgements of the importance of the moral question onto which Hamlet's psychological problem is fastened. The moral question is the substructure for Hamlet's conduct. Claudius has wrenched his time, like a shoulder bone, out of joint. Hamlet never doubts that it is his task to be moral doctor and "set it right". There is a moral basis in his insistence on the importance of godlike reason and in his labelling the murders "madness", an inversion of the true rationality which makes men moral beings. His misery is that he has to share in that madness. It is not the immorality of his task which drives Hamlet to distraction but the immorality of the world.

Tracing the outline of Hamlet's mentality, an edifice of human complications set in a moral substructure, is a lengthy process. Many hints are hidden in terms such as "conscience", "blood", "action", "judgement" and "scourge" which need careful definition. The whole play is a uniquely subtle and complex construction of words, on the basis of which we trace in our imaginations a sequence of events. This in turn should indicate to us something of what was in Shakespeare's mind in London in 1600 when he put the words together for the stage. The remainder of this introductory chapter therefore

18

attempts to define some of the play's key words and its architecture. The subsequent chapters attempt to approach the question of Hamlet's mind, first (in chapter 2) through its mirror opposite, the Claudian globe, before looking (in chapters 3 and 4) at Hamlet's distraction. Chapter 3 looks at the initial mingling of moral and psychological pressures, judgement and blood. Chapter 4 looks at its development around the pivotal point of the play, Hamlet's impulsive murder of Polonius, which commits him irrevocably to the choice of blood. Chapter 5 attempts to put all this analysis into perspective with a scene-by-scene study of the events in sequence.

II

One of the lesser marvels of *Hamlet* is how neatly the minutest details tally with the structure as a whole. Single words and phrases unerringly reflect the pattern of the drama in which they are set, as the single head of Hamlet reflects the world he inhabits. This confronts the modern reader with an obvious initial difficulty, since many of his key words have lost some of their meanings since his day. We may note, for instance, that Hamlet insists on using the word "conscience" where we might expect, after Montaigne, that he would use "justice". That usage would seem less significant if we did not know the link between conscience as moral awareness and the "reason" (moral thought) which Hamlet regards as man's highest gift. Claudius has a bad conscience; Hamlet has a good one, but a conscience which means his ability to think morally, not just one free of guilt for wrongdoing, a "clear" conscience in our sense. The cowardice which he accuses himself of in all three of the soliloquies he delivers after learning the ghost's message is the outward appearance of an inward moral scruple, the "conscience" or thinking power which "doth make cowards of us *all*", because we all have that power if we care to use it.

The gulf between outward appearance and inward reality also yawns in a pair of key words, action and passion. Like "acting" action was playing with words, an appearance, the

19

outward performance of the actor's inward feeling. "Passion" was the passive feeling actively expressed in voice and gesture. For the professional actor or "player" acting was the pretence of an inward feeling, a deception. Because he assumes the First Player's passion in his Pyrrhus speech to be feigned, Polonius is disgusted when it brings tears to the speaker's eyes. Actors on stage were playing games, feigning their passionate fictions ("but in a fiction, a dream of passion" says Hamlet dismissively of the Player's tears), making a joke of painful realities. Murder on stage is only "tragedy played in jest" as Richard Crookback calls it (*3 Henry VI*, II.iii.28). The "action" of Claudius murdering old Hamlet as Hamlet re-enacts it in the 'Mousetrap' play is "poison in jest" (III.ii.221). The Greek name for an actor, hypocrite, is wholly appropriate to Claudius's "pious action". Passion and action, playing and doing, words and deeds, these between them make up the most pervasive metaphor of the play, itself an enactment of words, a pretence of reality, Hamlet's third meaning for "distraction".

Other key words, especially "seeming", follow the pattern of the play metaphor, and will be examined in detail later on. The words which accrue to "conscience" — reason, judgement, blood, scourge — will also be examined in context at a later point. At this preliminary stage it is more useful to look at other details to see something of Shakespeare's methods. Realism, in the use of credibly human characters and thoroughly complex human motivation, is the mode through which *Hamlet* is primarily conceived and presented. Its intricate complexity though includes many linkages of details which relate to the whole structure in ways usually called poetic or symbolic. Seemingly casual hints or references link with each other and confirm how taut the whole creation is. And each such linkage helps to clarify the main structure. Just a few of them will provide an outline for the public and private globes in Hamlet's head.

Destiny controls our ends, says Hamlet in Act 5, preparing his mind for the death to come. A little time before, at the beginning of the final Act, we heard the gravedigger tell us that he has been employed at his trade for thirty years. As he digs the first of the graves for the play's chief characters he says he started work the day Hamlet was born. Destiny, it seems, knows our ends.

Another linkage is made in the same exchange between Hamlet and the gravedigger, by the confirmation that Gertrude's marriage to Claudius followed thirty years of marriage to old Hamlet. That length of time is otherwise only registered in the Mousetrap play, when the Player King emphasises his thirty years' marriage with the Player Queen. We have no prior knowledge why thirty years is significant. The gravedigger's confirmation that the Player was referring to Gertrude's first marriage shows in retrospect how neat was the trick Hamlet played with the Mousetrap. He lulled Claudius into thinking the playlet was only another diatribe against his mother's "o'erhasty marriage" before springing the murder on him.

Claudius in his first appearance in the play drinks publicly, advertising his love of carousing. Hamlet disapproves: it is a Danish custom more honorable to break than to observe. Gertrude however won't see anything wrong in her new husband's conduct. These details make it plausible first that Claudius should think of a poisoned drink as his contingency plan to make sure Hamlet will die in the duel, then that Hamlet should refuse it, and finally that Gertrude should take it up instead. The sequence of events in Act 5 is prepared in Act 1.

Another piece of preparation for the duel slips out from Hamlet himself. Warned that he hasn't much chance he waves the fear aside, saying casually that he should be a match for Laertes because he has been practising since Laertes left to return to Paris. A curiously lucky chance, we might think, until we remember that Hamlet had learned the ghost's story that same night and so acquired a far more urgent reason to practise his swordsmanship.

Ophelia's disaster stems from the doubt shared by her father and brother whether she would be an acceptable partner in marriage for Hamlet, since he is the heir apparent. Claudius proclaims Hamlet his heir in I.ii. In I.iii Laertes and Polonius both warn Ophelia to hold Hamlet off because he is a prince "out of thy star". She consequently returns Hamlet's gifts and gives him thereby a reason to display his lunatic disposition. Polonius jumps to the conclusion that Hamlet is mad because his love was rejected, and dies because he is still trying to spy on Hamlet to prove his theory when Hamlet has moved on from acting to action. Only when father and daughter are both dead does Gertrude casually prove the original doubt to have no foundation when she tells the corpse of Ophelia that she had hoped to see her married to Hamlet.

The laws of the Danish succession, the system of electing kings which lets Claudius freely choose who to give his "voice" or vote for, and which makes it possible for him to appear in law a legitimate king and not a usurper are also explicitly sketched in. Claudius is an elected ruler, so Polonius and the other servants of state are acting properly, within the limits of their grasp of the situation, in giving loyal service to him. Polonius is an honest spy, acting in his country's interest so far as he knows.

Shakespeare also played around with characters' names. He changed the king's name from Fengon to Claudius for reasons which illuminate Hamlet's reference to Nero at III.ii.367. Nero, nephew to the incestuous Roman emperor Claudius, murdered not his stepfather-uncle but his mother. Rosencrantz and Guildenstern are also Shakespeare's embellishments. Both are Danish names found in contexts which like the Claudius-Nero link offer curious parallels to Hamlet's story. In 1567 Eric Ottesen Rosenkrantz, Governor of Bergen Castle in the kingdom of Denmark, took Bothwell prisoner after his escape across the North Sea. Bothwell, husband of Mary Queen of Scots, was in flight largely because of his murder of Darnley, Mary's first husband. A Morgens Gyldenstjerne (or Gullunstarne) was named as one of the witnesses to Bothwell's alleged deathbed confession of regicide in which he exonerated Mary from complicity in her husband's murder.[8] Gertrude, we take it, was not guilty of complicity either.

Over and above the individual details and linkages stands the play as a piece of dramatic action. Its architectural shaping is as fine as its detailing. It moves in two basic phases, what might be called the phase of Hamlet's passion and the phase

22

of his action. These cut across the traditional five act structure which organises the main pattern of events. The five act structure follows a clear sequence: in Act 1 the situation is laid out and Hamlet learns his task; in Act 2 suspicion and doubt grow as everyone spies on everyone and probes for truth under the general dissembling; in Act 3 suspicions are put to the test, and their confirmation in the Mousetrap play together with the ghost's second visit alters the impetus from passion (or the "acting" of passion) to action. Act 4 contains the early stages of action, and its first consequences, and Act 5 shows the final onset of action and its resultant deaths. The changes from suspicion to action in Hamlet, Claudius and Polonius don't all happen at the same time. When Claudius moves from spying to action in Act 2 Polonius lags behind. He is still spying when Hamlet kills him, some time after Claudius has decided that Hamlet is dangerous and must be sent away. Claudius is always a step ahead of everyone, including Hamlet, in plotting, but his plots come all from the same mould while Hamlet's develop with ultimately a better sense of the situation and the kind of action it calls for. Such overlapping between the main actors, together with the contrast of Claudius's quick and resolute decisions against Hamlet's slow and thoughtful build-up, give the play much of its sense of urgency, of crowded events always pressing onward.

Along with the patterning of dramatic action goes an equally precise structuring through patterns of parallels and contrasts, of character and situation. Hamlet is parallelled by Fortinbras and Laertes, all revenging sons of dead fathers. The Hamlet family is matched by the Polonius family: both fathers haunt their sons, one literally, the other with spies. Innocent Ophelia counterbalances frail Gertrude; the taciturn university friend Horatio counterbalances the wordy Rosencrantz and Guildenstern. Hamlet praises Horatio as a model of judgement, no pipe for fortune's finger, and in the next scene mocks Rosencrantz for trying to play him like a recorder. Later Horatio stands quietly at Hamlet's side while he mocks Osric, the chough in peacock's clothes spacious in land and words. In the duel Osric seconds Laertes, both wordy men like their master Claudius, while student Horatio seconds student Hamlet.

The central characters form a double pattern. The love triangle of old Hamlet, Gertrude and adulterous Claudius turns into the hate triangle of Claudius, Gertrude and avenging Hamlet. Claudius as murder victim takes the place of old Hamlet, the original murder victim, and Hamlet takes Claudius's place as murderer. Hamlet himself elaborates this parallel with the literary analogues of Troy's revenging Pyrrhus and Italy's poisonous Gonzago, as we shall see in more detail later. Ophelia in her madness draws parallels too, with songs and flowers, when she muddles her dead father with a dead lover and sees her lover as forsaking her and as a wandering pilgrim. Laertes' revenge too becomes the image of Hamlet's own cause, in Hamlet's eyes, another outbreak of the general infection. And Hamlet of course consistently contrasts himself to Hercules. At I.ii.153, before the ghost's task is put upon him, it is a simple contrast, scholar against man of action. In the "distracted globe" reference the scholar has been thrust into the man of action's role. By V.i.272-3 Hamlet can mock Hercules as the Laertes-like enemy, the thoughtless warrior helpless to prevent the fate in store for him.

Let Hercules himself do what he may,
The cat will mew, and dog will have his day.

Hamlet's opposition is Herculean, and he is going to beat it.

The Hercules references are to some extent markers for Hamlet's progress. Other markers of this kind appear too, especially at the beginning and end of the play, as if inviting us at the end to throw our minds back to the beginning and so measure the gulf that has been crossed. Ophelia's mad talk of withered violets, for instance, echoes Laertes' warning that Hamlet's vows of love are transient violets (I.iii.8). Laertes dying caught in his own trap "as a woodcock to mine own springe" (V.ii.287) echoes his father's dismissal of Hamlet's vows to Ophelia as "springes to catch woodcocks" (I.iii.115). Similarly the carousing saluted by drum and cannon, military noises, in I.ii. echoes fatally in V.ii. when the king drinks to

24

Hamlet's success in the duel. And Claudius as "the Dane", i.e. king and exemplar of Denmark, at I.ii.44 and 69, is challenged by "Hamlet the Dane" at V.i.239. "The Dane" is Claudius during the first phase, of passion. Hamlet is the Dane in the second phase, the phase of action which begins when he kills Polonius.

Finally we should note how in the larger patterning of the play the sequence of events is packed with ironies as each scene reflects on its predecessor. A scene in which Hamlet enjoins temperate "action" on the players is immediately followed by displays of highly intemperate action on his own part. Mad Ophelia enters with flowers in contrast with her bloodthirsty brother. But these ironies, and the place of all the details in the structure of the play, require the more spacious treatment of the next chapters.

Chapter 2

THE CLAUDIAN GLOBE

Based on an ostensible realism as the play is, the first subject to study, the framework of the action, is the Claudian world, the official, public world where appearances belie reality, and from which consequently Hamlet feels alienated. We begin with the court at Elsinore.

Shakespeare was always careful with his anachronisms. In the political background to his Elsinore story he carefully specifies the historical details and makes it clear that he is doing so. Any anachronisms in his presentation are at risk more from our misreading than his casualness. On the question of succession to the Danish throne for instance, where too many editors have assumed that hereditary succession by primogeniture, the automatic inheritance through the eldest son, was the norm, Shakespeare is careful to describe it as elective. A much older form in Europe than primogeniture, formalised by Charlemagne, election of kings by a council of elders was the standard procedure across medieval Europe, and certainly the normal practice in the ninth or tenth-century Denmark of the historical Amleth. Automatic succession by the eldest son did not replace election in England until 1272, in France in 1270, and later still in the less powerfully nationalistic territories such as Denmark.

One of the advantages of election was that it gave scope for the crowning of any eligible member of the royal dynasty if for any reason the heir apparent was unfit. A brother could rule if the eldest son was still a child, or a younger son if the eldest was an idiot. Normally the eldest son could expect to be elected, but not automatically. He was truly the "apparent" heir to the throne. The system had its problems, since an elected brother might well promote the claims of his own child ahead of the dead king's infant son, and the in-fighting where an infant or imbecile heir did exist was usually fatal to

26

someone. Five and more centuries of such struggles led in the end to a general preference for the automatic succession of the eldest son, whoever and whatever he might be, and consequently the elevation of primogeniture to the status of a law of nature, a law assumed to be ordained by God for the regulation of all mankind.

Looking back from an age which had found its kings through primogeniture with some degree of success for three hundred years, sixteenth-century writers were conscious of the hazards of the older system. Shakespeare dealt with the hazards of primogeniture in nine history plays. Election offered opportunities for even more mayhem of the kind exemplified in the Amleth story. It had the advantage for this play of clearing out of the way any direct concern for title, the problem handled so extensively in the history plays. Hamlet's problem is personal, not dynastic. His mayhem does not come from a struggle for power. Shakespeare used anachronisms in Denmark, but not over the Danish constitution.

The details of Denmark's elective system are touched in obliquely but fully. We are first given a hint in the parallel case of Norway, which also settled on its kings by election. At I.i.80-104 Horatio tells the story of the wager between the now-dead King Hamlet of Denmark and his opposite, old Fortinbras of Norway, and how young Fortinbras wants to regain the lands lost when his father was killed by old Hamlet. Not for another hundred lines, till I.ii.28-30, do we learn (and then in passing) that the new king of Norway is not young Fortinbras but the dead king's brother, "uncle of young Fortinbras". The parallel between Denmark and Norway is thus made clear. We know the Danish situation by now since Claudius began his speech from the throne with a reference to "Hamlet our dear *brother's* death".

Several niceties of the election system are touched on in the same scene. Claudius emphasises at the beginning of his opening speech that both his accession to the throne and his marriage were approved by the council. "Nor have we herein barred / Your better wisdoms, which have freely gone / With this affair along." Again, when he addresses the dead king's

27

son as "our cousin Hamlet and *my* son", he is taking care to claim a closer kinship than young Fortinbras has to his uncle the king of Norway. By marrying the queen Claudius has avoided the problem of choice between the dead king's heir and any children of his own. He confirms this implication of his marriage a few lines later when he explicitly announces that young Hamlet is his choice as the next king.

> You are the most immediate to our throne . . .
> Our chiefest courtier, cousin, and our son.

This is the "pledge" to which he announces he will drink that night. He has made as decisive an announcement as Hamlet's own at the end of the play when he declares that Fortinbras "has my dying voice" in the election of a new king (V.ii.338). That the king's pledge has been registered is confirmed when Rosencrantz reminds Hamlet that "you have the voice of the king himself for your succession in Denmark" (III.ii.318-9). With the king's own vote in his pocket Hamlet's election is as nearly guaranteed as any question of power can be. The same pledge leads Laertes and Polonius in the next scene to warn Ophelia that Hamlet is a prince out of her star.

Claudius's pledge has far-reaching consequences. Laertes says Ophelia has to reject Hamlet's love because it can only be lust. Marriage is out of the question because Hamlet's consort will be chosen by the advice and consent of his council — "circumscribed / Unto the voice and yielding of that body / Whereof he is the head." In his choice of human flesh, says the gentle brother, Hamlet being royal may not "Carve for himself." How exalted and guarded Hamlet must be as heir apparent is constantly implied, when the queen calls him "our hope" (II.ii.24) or when Claudius sensibly comments "Madness in great ones must not unwatched go" (III.i.187). And yet the question of the succession is open enough for Claudius to offer it to Laertes and for the mob to riot on his behalf.

> The rabble call him lord;
> And, as the world were now but to begin,
> Antiquity forgot, custom not known,

28

The ratifiers and props of every word,
They cry, 'Choose we; Laertes shall be king!'

(IV.v.98-102)

Custom demands that the council elect him, not the mob. But no custom, even the custom of carousing to his pledge, will hold Claudius to his vote for Hamlet if expediency makes it convenient to offer it to Laertes instead.

Election runs continually in Hamlet's mind. He calls Horatio his soul's "elected" friend (III.ii.60), and his thwarted ambition is one of the three charges he puts up against Claudius, the only one he feels free to declare publicly. In the closet scene to Gertrude he calls Claudius a cutpurse who has stolen the crown. To Ophelia he describes himself — a public and not undissembling statement — as "very proud, revengeful, ambitious" (III.i.125). Rosencrantz in his clumsy attempt to pick up Hamlet's thinking had already used the last word (II.ii.249). Hamlet even does him the convenience of returning it to him (III.ii.317) in reply to a direct question over the cause of his "distemper". Saying he lacks advancement is what he knows his audience expects him to say. But election is in his mind, and there is an element of truth in the admission. In V.ii.65, when he rehearses the list of Claudius's crimes to Horatio, he makes the point explicitly and unambiguously. Claudius has not only "killed my king and whored my mother" and plotted against Hamlet's own life, but has "Popp'd in between th'election and my hopes".

Hamlet's hopes were not only hopes of power for himself. Even before he learns of the murder Claudius committed to gain the throne he is bitter about the new king. In the first soliloquy after he has seen Claudius at his smooth work Hamlet's comparison of dead king to living king carries with it the assumption that Claudius degrades the throne, that there is an honour in the post, an ideal of conduct to which Hamlet himself aspires and which is out of Claudius's reach.

My father's brother, but no more like my father
Than I to Hercules!

(I.ii.152-3)

Hamlet is disgusted with the Claudian world well before he knows it to be a criminal one. Between the Hamlet world and the Claudian world there is an unbridgeable gulf; they are alternative societies.

The Claudian world is a practical one, and within its own terms markedly more successful than the Hamlet world in maintaining law and order, peace and prosperity in the land. Claudius fights with superb skill and resolution for the security of his "state", a word which encompasses his prosperity, his throne, and his kingdom. Like his travesty Polonius Claudius uses the cunning of age against the rashness of youth. All the threats, a balanced group of challenges, come from the younger generation. Young Fortinbras threatens invasion from abroad; young Laertes threatens rebellion from within; and beyond both of these public dangers is young Hamlet, a secret cause of insecurity both to the king's title and his life. A king who poisons people through their ears manages to defeat two of the threats, the external and the internal, with mere words; he even turns them to his own advantage. Throughout the play Claudius acts with speed and sureness to avert every risk, in a masterly display of political skill. His only failures are in his first plot against Hamlet's life once the threat comes into the open, and in the excess of cunning which this failure draws him on to, what you might call his overkill, in the final scene. At the very end, too, his loyal courtiers do not come when he calls on them for help against Hamlet. He is more alone then than Hamlet himself.

The details of Claudius's manoeuvres are sketched in lightly but fully, and the skeleton of the plot can be seen in them. Claudius initiates every action in the play except the murder of Polonius and Ophelia's suicide. We can trace the whole sequence of events through Claudius.

The first detail is the guarded battlements and preparations for war. Sentries, two of whom we meet at the opening of the play, are on constant watch; armourers and ship-builders are working overtime (their "sore task/Does not divide the Sunday from the week"). The defences are alert because young Fortinbras is planning to invade Denmark, unknown to his old uncle

30

the king of Norway, to regain lands his father lost to Hamlet's father. A thoroughly serious threat against which Claudius is making serious defensive preparations.

In the scene of the king in council which immediately follows, however, we find him doing more than passively wait for the invasion. The first item on the agenda after the formal words about his predecessor and his marriage is an announcement that the threat of invasion is to be met by sending ambassadors to warn the Norwegian king of his nephew's plan, in the hope that old Norway will honour the agreement over Denmark's annexation of the land and so prevent Fortinbras from trying to regain it. Claudius is in total command of the situation. He trusts himself to assess the danger accurately and to judge the best action to take. He keeps a firm grip on events – the ambassadors are to deliver his written message to the Norwegian king and no more. Eventually of course (in II.ii) we shall hear that his judgement was right and that the stratagem has succeeded. The invasion is stopped without bloodshed and at minimal cost to Denmark.

The next two items on the council's agenda at this first meeting (I.ii) are seemingly trivial domestic matters. They do however have a bearing on state security too, and Claudius well knows it. The first item is Laertes' request for permission to return to the high life of Paris after his dutiful attendance at the funeral and wedding festivities, which Claudius readily grants him. The Claudian world approves of courtly training in Paris as it does of deep drinking at Elsinore. The second item is Claudius's refusal of permission for Hamlet to return to his studies at Wittenberg. Diplomatically he gives the reason that Hamlet is important to the state as the nominated successor to Claudius. This piece of candy he injects with the tart suggestion that as heir apparent Hamlet really ought to learn to behave better and dress more normally. When Hamlet's response is insultingly to ignore Claudius and reply only to his mother Claudius chooses to gloss it over ("'tis a loving and a fair reply"). He has got his way in the important matter, that of keeping Hamlet where he can be watched. And he has put Hamlet in the wrong simply by displaying his own tact and

31

discretion in contrast with Hamlet's surly offensiveness. Hamlet's attitude is anything but the "gentle and unforced accord" which Claudius chooses to call it, as everyone at court can witness, to Hamlet's shame. Only Hamlet sees the iron hand behind the smooth reproof. Denmark's a prison, he tells Rosencrantz later.

Claudius's final words to his council are image-builders too. He is hearty, carousing, carefree. "No jocund health that Denmark drinks today, / But the great cannon to the clouds shall tell, / And the king's rouse the heaven shall bruit again." Not for him the lean and hungry look. He is richly dressed (a peacock Hamlet calls him), and a hearty drinker who can dissemble enough to poison other people with it when need be.

Not that Hamlet, out of step as ever, is above accusing Claudius of thrift ("the funeral baked meats / Did coldly furnish forth the marriage tables" I.ii.179-80). That is a mark of Claudius's inversion of values, like the drinking, which Hamlet also condemns at I.ii.174 and I.iv.8-22. Claudius's choice of drink as a concealment for his mental sharpness, his disguise for the solitude that the possession of power entails, leads Hamlet into his "mole of nature" speech, about men who suffer condemnation in general for one vice in particular. Since that is not at all Claudius's situation, Hamlet's criticism says more about his antipathy to Claudius, his rejection of the king's way of making himself seem human, than it does of Claudius's standing in the community at large. In outward appearances Claudius wins hands down. His behaviour is impeccable, his policy sound and economical, his handling of an ungracious and hostile stepson discreet and effective.

Claudius next appears in Act 2, after Hamlet has learned the ghost's story and has resorted to his "antic" (clowning) disposition as his own form of image building. Claudius, ever cautious and alert to possible dangers, won't take what he calls this "transformation" at face value and has fetched two of Hamlet's "school fellows", fellow-students from Wittenberg, to spy on him and find what lies behind his strange behaviour. He is sceptical of Polonius's conjecture that Hamlet is merely love-sick, but agrees to test it as an additional line of investigation. The ambassadors have returned from Norway with Fortinbras's invasion successfully scotched, so Claudius is free to turn his full attention to what is clearly developing as the next threat to state security.

Hamlet of course has no trouble baffling both his fellow students and Polonius, so that early in Act 3, when Claudius gets their reports on what they have found he can see that they will never get anywhere. Consequently after he has himself spied on Hamlet's antic behaviour to Ophelia his conclusions are properly cautious, and his decision prompt.

> Love! His affections do not that way tend;
> Nor what he spake, though it lacked form a little,
> Was not like madness. There's something in his soul
> O'er which his melancholy sits on brood;
> And I do doubt the hatch and the disclose
> Will be some danger; which for to prevent,
> I have in quick determination
> Thus set it down: he shall with speed to England,
> For the demand of our neglected tribute.
>
> (III.i.161-69)

Such a mission is proper for a prince. Moreover a sea voyage, he tells Polonius, might help to clear that distracted head. But the Mousetrap, Hamlet's essay at spying, is waiting for Claudius, and when it snaps shut Claudius sees that the egg Hamlet is sitting broodily on (164-5) does indeed contain something dangerous. Before it can hatch therefore Hamlet must be sent away. Claudius is ahead of Hamlet here too. Even before Hamlet has finished his turn at spying Claudius has shifted from suspicion to action, in a prompt and sensible reversal of his earlier decision to keep Hamlet at court where he could be watched. In III.iii Claudius, quickly back in control after the "distemper" which Hamlet's Mousetrap play put him in, orders Rosencrantz and Guildenstern to escort him overseas on the grounds that his lunacy and his closeness to the royal family puts the throne in danger.

> The terms of our estate may not endure
> Hazard so near us as doth hourly grow

Out of his lunacies.

(III.iii.5-7)

A thoroughly reasonable precaution. Unfortunately Claudius's helpers are less prompt than he is. Polonius is still intent on spying, and worse still Gertrude has roused herself to take an initiative. Stirred to action for the first time on seeing the way her son used the Mousetrap to provoke her new husband, she decides to speak to him, to tell him off as if he were an ill-behaved child. When he replies with very unchildlike violence, and holds her in her seat to listen to his sharp words, she remembers the violence of lunatics and shrieks for help, with results fatal to her would-be helper behind the curtain, who is also too frightened to do anything but stay where he is and cry for help. On hearing of this catastrophe Claudius, fresh from his attempt to repent his brother's murder, decides that his stepson must be destroyed to prevent more trouble.

Polonius's death is a potential disaster which Claudius can easily turn to his own advantage. He can hold Hamlet prisoner (in the Kozintsev film Hamlet was put in a strait-jacket) till he is safely on board ship for England, and even has a potential excuse for making sure that Hamlet never returns alive. To Gertrude he can explain shipping him off as getting him out of the way till the uproar over the "vile deed" has blown over. He has to do something because he will in any case be blamed for failing to keep mad Hamlet where he could do no harm, and by sending him away he might be able to escape the slanders which would be bound to grow if he did nothing to check his errant son and heir.

In IV.vii, moreover, Claudius admits a further difficulty, that besides the problem of upsetting his doting mother Hamlet's popularity with the people makes it difficult to "put the strong law on him". So to Hamlet and the immediate court he announces that the reason for sending Hamlet overseas is for Hamlet's own safety. His soliloquy announcing the secret reason, that Hamlet is to be killed while away, follows immediately. We can take it, presumably, that Claudius has inserted this further twist of policy into the original plan as a result of

34

Hamlet's murder of Polonius, though it might equally well be a result of the Mousetrap's revelation that Hamlet knows about his father's murder. I think we should take it that after the Mousetrap at first Claudius is genuinely penitent, and that only the ominously short work Hamlet makes of Polonius, a surrogate for the king, pushes him into the decision to kill him. Expediency forces him into more and more devious turns as the pressure of Hamlet's threat to his security mounts.

Turning Polonius's murder to his advantage in this way is adroit enough, but there are other troublesome consequences of the deed, in Polonius's orphaned children, which call for even more speedy footwork. The furtive burial of the corpse was necessary to keep the queen believing in her husband's desire to protect Hamlet, but it causes problems with both children. Ophelia's madness is obviously Hamlet's fault, another item in his crime sheet, but the burial does make it seem that Claudius is protecting Hamlet. It is therefore some sort of pretext for Laertes to raise his rebellion on. "We have done but greenly, / In hugger-mugger to inter him" (IV.v.79-80), admits Claudius. He already knows of Laertes' return and the rumour-mongering which is stirring up a general suspicion against him as king: "necessity, of matter beggared, / Will nothing stick our person to arraign / In ear and ear" (IV.v. 88-90). There is evidently popular support for Hamlet's invidious comparison of Hyperion-Hamlet to his satyr-brother. Claudius does not command the universal respect his brother had.

But Claudius is a man for all occasions. Just as he stopped the invasion by Fortinbras with a word in old Norway's ear, so now he stops Laertes' insurrection with words, and turns one enemy against another by diverting Laertes' passion against Hamlet. Claudius is at his best in the scenes with Laertes because we know for the first time exactly what he has to cope with and see him doing it. He is cool, steady, ripe with the native hue of resolution, a perfect actor of a part he knows to perfection. Supremely disingenuous, reminding Gertrude in passing that her son is "most violent author / Of his own just remove", he uses her when Laertes bursts in as a foil to his

35

own brave stand. He draws Laertes from violence into an exchange of words, and once on his own ground sets to work to adjust him from a blind to a precisely aimed hatred.

> That I am guiltless of your father's death . . .
> It shall as level to your judgement 'pear
> As day does to the eye.

(IV.v.146-9)

He knows perfectly what the outward appearance of events will show.

> Make choice of whom your wisest friends you will,
> And they shall hear and judge 'twixt you and me,

a judgement he gives a price to by putting his crown and life on it. His plan is clear: "Where th'offence is let the great axe fall". Laertes will learn that Claudius is already in the process of executing justice on Hamlet.

That of course can't happen in Gertrude's hearing, and only in IV.vii, once the judgement has been passed in Claudius's favour and Gertrude is absent, can Claudius describe the details of the execution. He explains that he hasn't punished Hamlet openly because the queen is so devoted to him and because of his general popularity, "the great love the general gender bear him". But Laertes may be satisfied.

> You must not think
> That we are made of stuff so flat and dull
> That we can let our beard be shook with danger
> And think it pastime.

The Mousetrap play, danger in pastime, evidently still rankles. And then just as Claudius is on the point of telling Laertes his plot to kill Hamlet comes the news of the prince's return. On hearing that calamity Claudius changes direction without a tremor. He wisely omits to tell Laertes that he's already tried to kill Hamlet once and has failed, and within a few seconds is offering Laertes the chance to do it himself with a new scheme which he ironically claims is "ripe in my device". Once again it has to be devious, to appease both Hamlet's partisans and his enemies.

> ... for his death no wind of blame shall breathe;
> But even his mother shall uncharge the practice,
> And call it accident.

So, resourceful as ever, Claudius manoeuvres Laertes into position with that implausible account of Hamlet's jealousy over Laertes' reputation as a swordsman. Italianate poisons are added to the French notion of a duel (Claudius evidently has less faith in Laertes' swordsmanship than he lets Laertes know), and the plan for Laertes' revenge is ready.

The two contrasting scenes about death, Ophelia's suicide and the gravedigging scene, hold us off until the plan is ready to be set in motion. When Hamlet and Laertes fortuitously meet at the graveside and fight, Claudius tells both Laertes and Gertrude to have "patience", for opposite reasons. Still playing the game both ways, Claudius says confidently to Gertrude when they learn of Ophelia's suicide that he'd only just managed to cool Laertes down, and that the news would set him on his path of revenge again.

That note, the ambiguous voice of the seemingly well-meaning diplomat, sounds again at the outset of the duel when Claudius, having laid his fatherly bet on Hamlet, makes the contestants shake hands and declare a truce to animosity. Even in the scuffle when the poisoned foil cuts both of them he pretends peacemaking — "Part them. They are incensed." To the very end he keeps up his act. When Gertrude collapses poisoned by the drug meant for Hamlet he desperately declares "She swoons to see them bleed." But finally, when Laertes gasps out the truth and Hamlet swoops to his revenge, he is alone. His plea for help — "O, yet defend me, friends; I am but hurt" — goes unheeded. Words at last will not serve. They have substituted for general popularity only for so long as Claudius has remained conspicuously in control. Now, as his most complicated plot begins to go astray and strew more bodies on the stage, an action at last begins which only Claudius himself, face to face with Hamlet at last, can play. The final action belongs to the two most solitary figures alone.

This is the story of what happens in the play at its political,

Claudian level. Claudius is an *efficient* king, supremely competent at handling challenges to his state, external and internal alike. He is just in the routine performance of his rule, commanding the loyalty of the old king's chief counsellor and the allegiance of the court. There is no illegality in his being elected ahead of young Hamlet to the crown of Denmark; he cannot be challenged as an usurper. Marrying the former king's widow was useful to secure his position, but it is also obviously a love match of sorts on both sides, whether or not we take the ghost's allegation of adultery to mean a liaison preceding the murder. The only intractable problem in the way of a peaceful and prosperous rule is young Hamlet. And how childishly *he* behaves. Sulky, and solitary, he refuses to cast off his mourning clothes when the new king decrees that the proper period is over. He seems to enjoy the public contrast of his own gloomy black with the celebratory colours and deep-drinking of the court. He won't even concede the semblance of good manners towards the king, in spite of a promise that the king will give his support to Hamlet's succession. Openly hostile and ambitious in the eyes of the court, he becomes when afflicted by seeming insanity openly threatening. He insults the tender Ophelia as readily as he insults the king his stepfather. He assaults his mother and murders the chief counsellor of the state. He treats the corpse of his victim shamefully and shows little sign of penitence for his deed. He fights with the murdered man's son in the grave of the daughter, a tender girl driven to suicide by Hamlet's acts against her and her father. He insults even the seemingly well meaning Osric. He is utterly at odds with the court and his position in it. He is the only discordant note in the well orchestrated Claudian world.[1]

That, very roughly, is the sequence of political actions in the story of *Hamlet*. It is Claudius's story, the narrative of his struggle to maintain order and security in the state for which, as king, he has total responsibility. Kings kept order and administered justice, and in return their subjects owed obedience. Hamlet's disobedience ended in the total destruction of the royal family and dynasty, and the family of Denmark's chief

38

counsellor. On almost every count it is a story of political disaster caused by Hamlet alone.

Political collapse is what happens in the play on the Claudian level. Above it though is Hamlet's level, the region where all the major structural parallels and contrasts combine to focus attention not on Claudius as the centre of political events but on Hamlet. In the pattern of political challenges to state security Hamlet is in the centre, Laertes and Fortinbras on either flank, Claudius the target for all three, for reasons which emphasise the solitary eminence of Hamlet's perspective against the merely expedient calculations of all the others.

The parallels of Fortinbras and Laertes to Hamlet are precise, each one taking up a different aspect of Hamlet's situation. Young Fortinbras is in the same position in Norway as Hamlet is in Denmark, the king his father and namesake dead, his father's brother on the throne. Laertes is in the same position as Hamlet, too, in having a father killed, his murderer unpunished and a target for the son's revenge. The two unthinking men of action, "outstretched heroes", flank the doubt-ridden student prince who shares their problems but not their psychology.

A more complex set of parallels and contrasts putting Hamlet above Claudius can be found in the two triangular patterns already mentioned. The first, old King Hamlet, his murderer Claudius and his queen, is explicitly made by young Hamlet to match its successor, King Claudius, murdering Hamlet and the queen, by means of two groupings of literary figures, King Priam – revenging Pyrrhus – Hecuba, and Player King – Lucianus – Player Queen. This matching of roles is a complex exercise. It links Hamlet and Claudius as regicides, and so makes a love triangle (husband, wife, lover) into a political issue. It puts Hamlet into Claudius's shoes as criminal murderer, regicide, and in some sense a rival for Gertrude's affections. Where the obvious value of the Laertes – Fortinbras – Hamlet parallels lies in the emphasis they give to Hamlet's inert suffering of his shame and his ultimate triumph, the two triangular patterns put his task of revengeful murder into deeper focus. Brother Claudius has murdered King Hamlet

39

and married the queen out of political ambition and earthly love. Nephew Hamlet must murder King Claudius and yet not destroy the queen with grief. His dilemma is the moral one in the act of revenge, the difficulty of punishing an evil act without committing an exactly parallel act.

Hamlet's first literary analogy to this problem is the old account of Priam's murder by fell revenging Pyrrhus, who hesitates before his sword falls as he hears the walls of Troy collapse around him but still sets Hecuba to her grief and the narrator to his tears. In this first analogy to his situation Hamlet is more concerned to incite himself with revenging Pyrrhus's example than to dwell on the grief of Hecuba. She of course laments the death of old Priam as Gertrude so conspicuously did not for old Hamlet: a noble Trojan precedent for ignoble Denmark. But will Gertrude weep this time, when revenging Hamlet drops his sword on the old head of Claudius?

In his soliloquy following the speech about Troy Hamlet checks himself for such a self-indulgent use of literary precedents, and sets about preparing a better analogy for his situation. The analogy he sets up, his Mousetrap, the murder of Gonzago, follows the ghost's account of King Hamlet's murder by Claudius in all its details, including the thirty years' marriage, except one. Hamlet gleefully points out to the increasingly worried Claudius as the Mousetrap unfolds, that the Player King's murderer is "one Lucianus, *nephew* to the King". Just as brother Claudius had been positioned in the triangle as rival and murderer of King Hamlet, so now nephew Hamlet will position himself in the new triangle as murderer of King Claudius. Even to the extent of winning the queen's love from the king.

Hamlet's problem over this last point is neatly illuminated in a third analogy when, on the point of visiting Gertrude after the Mousetrap, Hamlet tells himself he will not have the heart of a Nero. This, the reason Shakespeare changed the name Fengon from his sources into Claudius, is an allusion to Tacitus's view that the Emperor Claudius in marrying Nero's mother Agrippina was committing incest. He was her uncle. And of course Nero murdered not Claudius but Agrippina.

The two sets of triangular relationships and their historical analogies are patterns making it clear that Hamlet son must emulate his uncle's sin in avenging his father's death. It has the neatness of an eye-for-an-eye justice. It is the pattern Hamlet father expects his son to follow as unquestioningly as Fortinbras and Laertes follow their revenges. And as before what stands in the way of direct accomplishment, of a precise parallelism, is Hamlet's mind, his better consciousness of the implications of the larger pattern of things.

A trio of young men all aim their revenges against Claudius and the security of his state. Young Fortinbras is after Claudius to avenge his father's loss and the territory which went with it. Young Laertes is ready to overturn the throne for its murky involvement in the cover-up of his father's murder. Claudius turns both aside from their vengeance, Fortinbras into a futile "fantasy and trick of fame" as Hamlet calls it, the classic method of taking out one's frustration on a secondary target, and Laertes is diverted into serving the king. Laertes for his pains is sickened by what he has to do so much that he loses his desire for revenge altogether and asks his victim to "exchange forgiveness with me". Fortinbras for his acquiescence gains a kingdom.

Between these two casual slaughterers stands Hamlet, more powerfully impelled to murder (by three offences to Laertes' one), pushed by the ghost where Fortinbras and Laertes struggle only for their notional honour. All the structural analogues, the triangles and the parallelisms, draw our attention firmly to Hamlet's mental problem and indicate some of the complexities of his situation. Unlike his peers he pauses. Like rugged Pyrrhus he hears Troy falling. He hesitates over obstacles where Laertes and Fortinbras see only a clear road. He diverts his passion onto secondary targets as he sorts out the tangle of morality and psychology in which he is caught. The whole interim of Hamlet's delay between the order to take revenge and its execution is the central matter of the play.

41

Chapter 3

HAMLET'S GLOBE
(1): BLOOD AND JUDGEMENT

Hamlet's own explanation for his delay is nothing more than "conscience", that enigmatic term which to Elizabethans implied without affirming the moral component in human reason. It is a word he uses several times in claiming that the task is uniquely his. He, the cuckoo in Claudius's comfortable nest, will destroy the parent bird, first cause of the world's distraction, as an act of personal conscience, not of justice. At the one point in the play when he might be expected to call his revenge an act of justice he deliberately refrains, choosing instead the word which makes the decision his sole responsibility. Once he finally confronts Claudius in the duel where he must die, says Hamlet, it will be an act not of perfect justice but of "perfect conscience".

Justice, or judgement, is a word Hamlet avoids using of his position. He praises the combination of judgement with blood (passion) in Horatio but seems to regard his own position as too stressful, the weight of blood too oppressive, for impartial judgement to balance it. So he rests his case on his conscience.

The word "conscience" occurs eight times in the play. On its first two appearances it means Claudius's guilt over his crime. Hamlet declares at the end of Act 2 that he'll "catch the conscience of the king" with his Mousetrap play, and soon afterwards in the next scene Claudius uses it in his aside when he is upset by a casual reference of Polonius about hypocrisy, how with "devotion's visage" and "pious action" we "do sugar o'er / The devil himself". This is in fact the first confirmation we are given that the ghost's word is right and that Claudius has any conscience to be caught. The full story of the load of guilt he carries on his conscience does not come until after the Mousetrap has been sprung, in the prayer scene at III.iii.36-72. After that we get no more word from Claudius except what

42

goes with devotion's visage and pious acting. He gives a splendid exhibition of that in IV.i. when he hears that Polonius has been killed by his stepson.

Alas, how shall this bloody deed be answered?
It will be laid to us, whose providence
Should have kept short, restrained, and out of haunt
This mad young man.

A godly providence indeed that could have anticipated such dangerous conduct in a prince. It was his love, his Christian charity, of course, which softened his attitude and caused such negligence.

But so much was our love,
We would not understand what was most fit;
But, like the owner of a foul disease,
To keep it from divulging, let it feed
Even on the pith of life.

Foul diseases (an image Claudius turns on Hamlet as Hamlet has applied it to Claudius) call for radical surgery. So the prince has to be cut out of the body politic and sent to England for his health. Confronted with the need for action Claudius has mastered his conscience without a second's hesitation and aligned himself with the Fortinbras's of the world.

The other character apart from Hamlet himself who turns out to have a conscience is Laertes. In rebellion he first announces that nothing will stop his revenge.

To hell allegiance! Vows, to the blackest devil!
Conscience and grace, to the profoundest pit!
I dare damnation.

(IV.v.128-30)

Young Laertes doesn't hesitate to leap into the posture which Hamlet father expected of his son. But Laertes backs down as Hamlet begins to move. Laertes' fury starts at its height and can only ebb. By the time he gets in front of his victim, sword in hand, that conscience which in IV.vii.1 Claudius can reckon to be firmly on his side is beginning to waver. Poisoned foil in

43

hand, two attempts to prick Hamlet already thwarted, "'tis almost against my conscience", he tells himself. His feeling is not quite squeamish enough to stop him doing the trick in a rather underhand way, taking Hamlet by surprise, in the next bout. It is enough though to let him, once wounded himself, conclude "I am justly killed with mine own treachery", and therefore tell the plot to Hamlet, blaming the king for it and asking forgiveness of his victim with his dying breath.

Claudius's conscience is plain unsalted guilt. Laertes' conscience congeals out of thoughtless fury cooling to a sense of honour and justice. Hamlet's conscience is, inevitably, more of a mixed grill than either. The "conscience" he first mentions in the soliloquy at III.i.83 is the habit of thinking precisely on the event, the moral awareness which despite the contrary evidence of Claudius and Fortinbras he reckons makes a coward of every man. Sunburnt men of action lose their colour through the indoor habit of contemplation, of sorting out right from wrong, a process which paralyses because of the complexities (thinking *too* precisely) which thought brings to mind.

Hamlet mentions his conscience twice more within the space of a few lines in V.ii. while describing his native resolution in despatching Rosencrantz and Guildenstern. In the meantime of course sunburnt Laertes and weather-beaten Fortinbras have shown him the hue of their resolution in pursuit of their revenges and their honour. Adopting callousness as the next best thing to thoughtlessness he dismisses his execution of his former fellow students – "They are not near my conscience" – though he must still plead for Horatio's reassurance that it is right to confront Claudius himself. A duel is the honest course.

> – is't not perfect conscience
> To quit him with this arm?

> (V.ii.67-8)

And where Laertes accepted damnation as the price worth paying for his revenge, Hamlet worries whether he would not be damned for failing to take his. He frames his last reference

44

to conscience as a question, and it rings with something less than total assurance. Hamlet still has to wait for more pressure to force him into action. Conscience is no ally to resolution.

Conscience is the moral end of the spectrum of thought which we are told insistently through the play is the quality which marks men out from the animals. Without reason, says pious Claudius, we are pictures of mere beasts, a view repeated in anguish by Hamlet in his final self-damning soliloquy at IV.iv.33–39.

> What is a man
> If his chief good and market of his time
> Be but to sleep and feed? A beast, no more.
> Sure, he that made us with such large discourse,
> Looking before and after, gave us not
> That capability and godlike reason
> To fust in us unused.

Nothing is good or bad, says Hamlet, but thinking makes it so. Thinking elevates men above beasts because it gives men the faculty to tell right from wrong. The dead King Hamlet's wife is worse than a beast because even a beast without the gift of reason would have mourned longer than she did. So man, the paragon of animals, lacking so woefully that pattern of conduct which should distinguish men and women from animals gives him no pleasure.[1]

Conscience, whether defined through Hamlet's words or our own, must be taken to be one of the highest fences impeding Hamlet's revenge. Even without the triangular pattern which fits Hamlet into Claudius's role as regicide we can see how studying the implications of his task blocks his progress. We do not take seriously his first explanation of his delay as mere animal mindlessness, but we pay careful attention to his version of the alternative:

> whether it be
> Bestial oblivion, or some craven scruple
> Of thinking too precisely on th'event –
> A thought which, quartered, hath but one part wisdom

45

And ever three parts coward —

(IV.iv.39–43)

Conscience is a stumbling-block, no part of the military baggage of a man of action. Laertes at the end moves closer in his pattern of parallels to Hamlet than Fortinbras — who prompted the self-reproach just quoted — ever does. Unlike the merely military Norwegian Laertes alters his position over revenge, moving in the opposite direction to Hamlet, away from revenge, and repenting his act as conscience stirs him. Fortinbras on the other hand, shown early in the piece as reluctant to abide by "all bands of law" (I.ii.24), remains a soldier of fortune, a royal Hotspur to the end. When Hamlet, dying, tosses him the throne of Denmark it is a gesture of hopelessness, of a man who knows that in princes action is more valued than conscience. There is some sense of Hamlet making reparation. He has wiped out a dynasty in the course of attacking the madness which infected it. But Fortinbras's conscienceless acquisition of the Danish throne, renewing the old militarist order of King Hamlet, is the last step in a process of reduction, of accommodation to earthly realities, which Hamlet began to accept with Polonius's death. It is a defeat for reason.

Reason is a word used almost obsessively through the play by both Hamlet and Claudius. Reasonable, practical Claudius uses it for his level of conduct, and as the pillar which keeps up appearances. Hamlet's continuing grief for his dead father, says Claudius, is "a fault to heaven, / A fault against the dead, a fault to nature, / To reason most absurd." Hamlet uses the word to mark the faculty which raises men above beasts. It is the faculty of moral consciousness the lack of which damns Claudius as bestial, and ultimately mad. Judgement and conscience are no part of the Claudian vision of a reasonable world. Words, the power of speech which goes with God's gift to man of god-like reason, are perverted in the Claudian court. They become the instruments of spying and dissembling, concealing the truth they ought to display. Honesty is Claudius's first victim.

The pit which Hamlet descends into on learning the ghost's story stands there between the two kinds of reason, the world of truth and the world of "reasonable" Claudius. Reason and speech, the voice of reason, have alternative functions for Claudius and for Hamlet. Claudius uses words as the instruments of his seeming. Hamlet's words are honest to the extent that we can find the keys to his problems in them if we look at them carefully enough.

Many of the speeches in the play are sententious, characters lecturing one another with varying degrees of honesty. Hamlet himself follows the court habit of using hendiadys, what Puttenham called the "figure of twynnes", in which two words of similar meaning occur where one might do or where one might qualify the other (Hamlet speaks of the "book and volume" of his brain; a bookish volume, a brain voluminously bookish, a capacious memory bank). Unlike the other wordy lecturers, however, Hamlet does it with a difference. His twinnings are not verbose; each word enhances the other (the motive and the cue, whips and scorns, circumstance and course of thought). On some key occasions they are directly antithetical to each other. The two most striking instances of this are the two phrases which go to the heart of his own problem of the two worlds: "blood and judgement" (III.ii.65), and "scourge and minister" (III.iv.176). Both occur in the centre of the play as Hamlet is coming to terms with his circumstance and his course of thought.

The first of them, blood and judgement, puts labels on the radical alternatives he is grappling with. Hamlet's blood, the passionate will which Laertes and Polonius warn Ophelia against in I.iii, is what summons him to his revenge. Black Pyrrhus in II.ii. is covered in heraldic blood: "head to foot / Now is he total gules". In III.ii. while waiting for his Mousetrap to start Hamlet praises Horatio for his balance.

> And blest are those
> Whose blood and judgement are so well co-mingled
> That they are not a pipe for fortune's finger,
> To sound what stop she please.

A little later, with double irony since Polonius lies dead at his feet, he tells his mother off for letting her blood govern her judgement. "At your age", he says, "The hey-day in the blood is tame, it's humble,/ And waits upon the judgment." By Act 4 Hamlet has conceded the victory in himself to his blood. Judgement ("That capability and god-like reason") has gone over to the side wanting revenge. Thought must throw off its pale cast, it must be bloody or be nothing worth. So his revenge is made doubly imperative by the "Excitements of my reason *and* my blood" (IV.iv.38–66). Conscience, the basis of judgement, has conceded the case for revenge.

The other special figure of twynnes, "scourge and minister", is another antithesis. It illustrates with utter concision how the polar opposites of reason and blood can turn into the horns of a dilemma and finally into a trap which will hold Hamlet until death. It also explains how judgement can join blood by Act 4 in urging revenge. But to expand these two antitheses from concise summaries into their full context in the play is perhaps going too fast. We need first to look closely at the antitheses of passion and action which are basic metaphors in the play, and the world of seeming, of false realities, in which they are set.

Reality is an object of continual suspicion in the play. From the first mention of the ghost, that apparition of which book-learned Horatio is at first properly sceptical, through Hamlet's whole parade of madness and self-mistrust, to the spying made necessary by doubts of all kinds, "seeming" and mistrust of people's seeming is the normal attitude of the prime movers in the play. Act 1 sets up a situation in which everyone has reason to doubt everyone else. The air is cold with mutual suspicion where everyone speaks less than he knows and believes less than he sees or hears. Claudius and Hamlet have good reason for mutual suspicion even before the ghost's visit. But innocent Ophelia too is warned not to take Hamlet at his word on no better grounds than that, being young, he is likely to be more lecherous than honourable.

Act 2 shows the suspicions at work. It opens with Polonius instructing his man Reynaldo to spy out Laertes' doings in

Paris and continues with Claudius ordering the same surveillance of his stepson. The rottenness in the stately throne of Denmark has infected normal human relations. The only sound contact is between Hamlet and Horatio, though even there Hamlet can doubt Horatio's word about the ghost, and withhold from him for a time the story the ghost had to tell. Free as Hamlet is from all contriving, as Claudius testifies, he sees the court fawning on the new king, serving corruption and spying for him in ways that debase human conduct and spread the rottenness throughout the Claudian world. "Honesty" is a word he throws six times at Polonius in II.ii., and six times more at Ophelia in III.i when he thinks she may be spying too. His schoolfellows are infected, likewise, and are slow to admit the truth even when faced openly with it. The hypocrisy of villains who smile has wrenched the time out of joint.

Spying is what everyone does in Acts 2 and 3. In the domestic scene which opens Act 2 Reynaldo is sent to find what men say of Laertes, his reputation not his honesty. Ophelia's sad story of Hamlet's visit to her, when he appeared like a ghost from hell, shows how spying compels disguise, the antic deception set up to conceal the real grounds of Hamlet's grief. In II.ii. Claudius turns out to have started spying long before, sending (to Wittenberg?) for Rosencrantz and Guildenstern to search Hamlet's mind. In the same scene Polonius's report of Ophelia's unhappy experience shows how reasonable the court assumes spying to be, in the interests of state security. Claudius calls their schemes "lawful espials" at III.i.32. Act 2 ends of course with Hamlet easily fending off Rosencrantz, Guildenstern and Polonius. The ease with which he outmanoeuvres Claudius's agents at this point is an early measure of his equal stature with Claudius as an adversary. The game, which is what it is at this point, is on Claudius's own ground and played to his rules, but still it only ends in a draw.

It is a drawn game because Hamlet's deception does not cloud the king's view of the threat he represents. Claudius doubts Polonius's facile assumption that Hamlet is mad out of estranged love so far as to say that Hamlet "puts on" his air of confusion. He concludes after spying on Hamlet's talk with

49

Ophelia that the cause of his melancholy is neither love nor lunacy, and is "something in his soul" as yet unknown but certainly dangerous. Not that Claudius is incapable of claiming that Hamlet is mad when it is convenient for him to do so, as at III.iii.1–2. Lying is the sane companion of spying and deception.

Hamlet's mother is also drawn into the spying game once the Mousetrap stirs her into action. She allows herself to be used as inquisitor, with Polonius as witness to Hamlet's replies. After that scheme has gone so disastrously wrong Hamlet tries to turn her round, warning her against allowing Claudius to worm the truth out of her "That I essentially am not in madness, / But mad in craft", a warning she pays some heed to, on the evidence of her behaviour to her husband at the beginning of IV.i. when she has to tell him that her son has killed Polonius. Her account of the killing and of Hamlet's penitence are not very close to the truth. So the web of deception extends itself.

By the end of Act 3 Claudius has had his warning, and Polonius has been killed. Spying out Hamlet's mind has therefore lost its point. Deception then becomes the chief weapon. Hamlet has been using it from the beginning of Act 2, of course, as his main counter to Claudius's opening gambit of keeping him where he could be watched. As a deception Hamlet's antic (clownish) disposition takes different forms according to the audience. Pretending an extreme and unorthodox fit of love madness to Ophelia is one red herring, a ploy framed as the most plausible reason for distraction offered to the person most receptive to it, since love was thought to be equal with too much study as the commonest cause of melancholy. To his school fellows Hamlet offers a different device, unmotivated "melancholy adust", a bookish disenchantment with all the world. Such misanthropy, the stock alternative to love as the cause of madness, he pretends is cause rather than effect of his circumstances. Though the diagnosis has enough truth in it to be plausible.

Rosencrantz and Guildenstern's counter ploy to the melancholy adust deception, the distracting entertainment of the

50

players, is well fitted to the mental disorder known today as manic depressiveness. Hamlet's response to this kind of treatment confirms that there was more truth in the melancholy adust device than in the pose that poor Ophelia sees. The players do excite a manic element in Hamlet, more than the pleasure of meeting his friends again, more even than the first arrival of Horatio. Just as there is a hint of truth in Hamlet's misanthropic pose, so there is more than a touch of self-deception in his wholehearted search for distraction in his encounter with the players (II.ii.309–506). The rugged Pyrrhus speech has parallels with his own situation, and in the end he recalls himself to his duty with his enquiry to the First Player about the *Murder of Gonzago*. Still, he rightly lashes himself in soliloquy at the end of the Act for his willingness to be diverted.

The Gonzago Mousetrap is Hamlet's shift from passive deception to active spying on Claudius, his riposte to the clumsy probing of Rosencrantz, Guildenstern and Polonius. But in the meantime Claudius has been active ahead of him. Even before the Mousetrap he has tested the love madness theory, discarded it, and decided to send Hamlet away where he will be less dangerous, a reversal of his previous decision to keep Hamlet where he could be watched which has been made necessary by the failure of his spies to get anywhere with their watching. Claudius is always a step ahead of Hamlet even before the Mousetrap brings the conflict into the open between them, and nowhere more intelligently than in his change of policy from spying to action. Whether he had it in mind at this early stage to add treachery to his action by having Hamlet murdered while away across the sea is doubtful. That was a later step in the escalation of his safety measures. But even at this stage of continuing uncertainty he was sure enough to act on his suspicion, unlike his antagonist. Hamlet's deception, the variably presented antic disposition, has aroused more suspicion than it has allayed. Claudius is too sharp. Once the Mousetrap has shut and the spying can be dispensed with, again it is Claudius who initiates the new mode of operation, plotting for murder. With the snapping of the trap the game is

51

not a "play" any longer. The contest is out in the open, and Claudius has the initiative.

If Hamlet had killed Claudius at this point in the play, in the prayer scene which follows the closing of the Mousetrap, when the first breach has appeared in the king's defences and his back is turned to Hamlet's sword, many things would be wrong. The fight has hardly begun. The game has just become real war for the first time. Hamlet knows he has a powerful adversary, a monster of great talent and ingenuity. By sheer luck, just as the challenge has been thrown down and the first moves of the real contest are beginning, Claudius slips and Hamlet finds himself with the chance to finish it before it has really started. He does not pause out of doubt, nor from a vicious desire to damn Claudius as totally as he can, which is what he tells himself is his reason for hesitating. Rather he pauses because to kill Claudius at this point would be a furtive and trivial act, a stroke of luck the converse of the one he describes to Laertes as playfully shooting his arrow over the house and hurting his brother. It would not acknowledge the stature of Claudius's misdeed nor the proper immensity of the struggle the two adversaries have started on. It would not be a duel, the ending which he expects. Out of respect for himself he cannot trivialise his task or the scale of Claudius's crime with a piece of fortuitous bloodletting. After the success of the Mousetrap Hamlet feels he is strong, knows he is a match for Claudius, and wants the fullscale struggle to prove it. His judgement still counterbalances his blood in the scales of this decision.

But events do not turn out as he expects. The king's surrogate Polonius dies in a thoughtless moment, the opposite of the hesitation with drawn sword we have just seen in the prayer scene. Too late for Polonius Hamlet comes to see that the action phase has replaced the phase of spying and deception. The corpse tells him that as readily as his ghostly father's reproof. "This man shall set me packing", he wryly notes (III.iv.212). With the killing of Polonius passion pivots into action and events move at increasing speed beyond the control of either of the principals in the duel.

Deception now works in the service of action. Claudius

deceives Gertrude, Laertes and all in his attempts to destroy Hamlet. Hamlet plays a devious part too. He poses again as lunatic to his guards, an act Claudius has no hesitation in exploiting. He feigns the ranting lover to Laertes and the compliant stepson to Osric, when Claudius wants to see his prowess with the rapier. The deceptions continue as Claudius pretends to Gertrude to be protecting Hamlet against his crime (IV.i.30-2), on the conveniently provided grounds of his madness, while in reality building up a case against him (IV.v.73, 76-7, 80 and in his presentation of the story to Laertes). In V.ii. when the plot to murder Hamlet is poised, Claudius smoothly acts the role of peacemaker, urging the combatants to shake hands and declare a truce. Even at the last he lies as he tries to dissemble the queen's collapse. Deception is the consistent hallmark of Claudian conduct throughout the play.

Deception of course is the name of the game of playing itself, and Hamlet acknowledges it. In one of the finest and most complex pieces of word-play in the whole work, Hamlet describes his labour and admits his delay in terms belonging to the theatre. Lapsed in time and passion, he delays by his inability to make the transition from words to deeds, from passion to action, from playing to murder. Given the motive and the cue, he needs "prompting" to give his passion voice not just in words but in action. He must shift from poison in jest, as he calls the Mousetrap, to poison in deed. He must act not in a play but in reality. The whole pattern of deception is summed up in the theatre metaphor of the soliloquy which ends Act 2.

Hamlet's initial aversion to putting his sword through Claudius is nowhere more apparent than in his use of words rather than action to express his passion, to vent his head of steam. Thought is his favoured weapon, passion replaces action, his "action" is a deception, an actor's part, until he takes the irrevocable step and murders Polonius. When the ghost first mentions murder Hamlet begs for the truth so that he may sweep to his revenge with "wings as swift / As meditation or the thoughts of love" (I.v.29-30), curious similes for speed. When

53

later he lambasts himself for idleness his complaint is that he mopes like a dreamer "and can *say* nothing". He puts it that way even though, having whipped himself up with name-calling ("bloody, bawdy villain! / Remorseless, treacherous, lecherous, kindless villain!") into a copy of the player's passion, he condemns it as whorelike, unloading his heart with words. The Mousetrap plan which follows is another play, another game, acting instead of action.

Thoughts serve as stand-ins for deeds in the next acts too. After chiding himself in the third soliloquy for allowing his indoor cast of thought to lose his enterprise's "name of action", although he has openly threatened the king, killed Polonius and spoken daggers to his mother, he still has to exhort himself in the last soliloquy with the ambiguous "O from this time forth / My *thoughts* be bloody or be nothing worth." That conjunction, though, bloody thoughts, is something of a novelty. Blood and judgement have not properly co-mingled until now. Bloody thoughts are the only admissible alternative to "bestial oblivion" if man's life is not to be made cheap as beasts'. So in the end, his acting done, true to his devotion to words Hamlet can insist that Horatio live on to tell his story.

By the end of the play Hamlet has translated acting, the expression of passion, into action, the movement of reality. He has gone beyond the action of playing, feigning, finding oblique vents for his passion and pastimes for his beating mind. He has cut through the vast running image of life as a trick, a theatrical deception, a game, a play, an act. And in doing so he has left behind him the Claudian world. The metaphor of action is grounded there, and Hamlet does not escape from his prison until he translates action from deception to reality.

Acting is what all Elsinore does. Amongst the wise saws and ancient instances Polonius delivers to his fleshpot-bound son (I.iii.59–80) are the standard rules for Claudian conduct. Never put into action any "unproportioned thought", he tells Laertes, never speak your thoughts. Like the subsequent warnings, to trust well-tried friends and suspect new ones, to be slow but thorough in quarrel, to listen more than speak, it sounds like a burlesque version of the fences Hamlet is going to have to erect around his conduct if he is to survive in Claudius's company.

"Our thoughts are ours, their ends none of our own", says the Player King sententiously (III.ii.201), perhaps quoting one of Hamlet's dozen or sixteen lines. Words and deeds, the "ends" of thought, are never under more than precarious control in Hamlet, despite his mastery of both in training and potential. In his training he has preferred the pen to the sword, and for three acts of the play he clings to his more familiar weapon. His first move after proving the ghost's word with the Mousetrap is to accept his mother's summons, not to initiate any action. He will "speak daggers to her, but use none" (III.ii.370), careful to avoid giving his words the seal of action (372-3). Gertrude first calls such behaviour a mere wagging of his tongue (III.iv.40) but by line 96 is saying that his words enter her ears like daggers, a reminder both of Hamlet's local intention with his mother and of his larger task, since the ear was where Claudius's poison entered. It takes the ghost's arrival a few lines later before he can turn from the local task to the larger, "thy almost blunted purpose". Hamlet pours truth, Claudius pours lies and poison into human ears, and Hamlet's is the less gainful exercise. Aiming his words at his mother is easier than aiming his sword at Claudius. Hers is the lesser crime, the lesser punishment, and Hamlet is more prac·tised with the instrument of her punishment, passion more than action. The ghost had expressly ordered him to leave Gertrude alone (I.v.84-8), and his defiance of the ban is a measure of how much easier he finds it to attack Gertrude with words than to face Claudius. Her veniality is an error which his sense of moral outrage picks at like an unhealed scar. Had he been less at ease with words and less bothered by murder he would have been less impelled to vent his passion on his mother.

Several times in the last two Acts words are described as poor substitutes for action. For Hamlet at IV.iv.22 (his letter to Horatio) words are now too light in calibre to fit the cannon of infamy which fights for Claudius. Claudius gives

Hamlet's words proof in the next scene as he diverts Laertes' revengeful purpose with his lies and puts to him Hamlet's own problem: "What would you undertake / To show yourself your father's son in deed / More than in words?" (IV.vii. 124-6). Following such a challenge it is ironically appropriate that Hamlet should find himself obliged to compete with Laertes in words before he faces him in deeds, sword at last in hand. At Ophelia's graveside he parodies the voice of Laertes' grief ("Nay, an thou'lt mouth, / I'll rant as well as thou" V.i.264-5), in a savage mockery of his own attempts at therapy by passioning in words.

Mouthing or exaggerating the "action" of a speech, like other breaches of verbal decorum, is always an irritant to Hamlet. Even his own mad speeches only "lacked form a little" (III.i.162) compared with the "nothing" (IV.v.7) of Ophelia's madness. His insistence that the players should not mouth their speeches shows also against Laertes, against Guildenstern ("Pronounce", he says ironically when reproved for not keeping his "discourse in some frame" at III.ii.289-91), against the player's "damnable faces" (III.ii.238), and against Fortinbras, who "makes mouths" at the future for the price of an eggshell. Along with the "frame" of a speech, and its appropriate action, pronunciation was the essence of good speaking, a concern of scholars, courtiers and players alike. It requires decorum as does action.

In its technical sense 'action' occurs in the play only in the first three Acts. The first use is perhaps the most striking of all because it launches at once all those associations, of acting with deception and of 'playing' as a substitute for reality, which help to make the word a continual reproof to the revenge-burdened prince. In I.ii., when Gertrude begs Hamlet to give up his mourning clothes for colours better suited to a cheerful future, he rounds on her for the assumption that feelings can be changed like clothes. His only speeches up to this point have been two monosyllabic punning lines taking up the ambiguities in other speakers' words. This time he picks up an unfortunate word of Gertrude's.

56

Seems, madam! Nay, it *is*; I know not 'seems'.
'Tis not alone my inky cloak, good mother,
Nor customary suits of solemn black,
Nor windy suspiration of forced breath,
No, nor the fruitful river in the eye,
Nor the dejected 'haviour of the visage,
Together with all forms, moods, shows of griefs,
That can denote me truly. These, indeed, *seem*,
For they are actions that a man might play.

(I.ii.76–84)

Any man could 'act' such shows of grief if they weren't real to him. Like the professional player who can bring tears to his eyes with his fiction by pretending the passion appropriate to his action, any man can find actions to match his words without reality or truth in either. This is the "pious action" of Claudian hypocrisy, and the "passionate Action" of the grieving player queen in the dumb show.

'Playing' too changes its meaning at the end. Claudius's behaviour is not much more than cheating at cards in the beginning, "foul play" (I.ii.254). Hamlet is employed in "pranks" as Polonius calls them (III.iv.2). It is all "false fire" (III.ii.250). So long as Hamlet is still "passion's slave" his actions are games, playing. His feelings, blocked from the kind of expression displayed freely in the player's "action", vent themselves through the clowning of his antic disposition, through his Mousetrap play, through games and "pastimes" which disperse his impulse towards the central action.

By Act 5 the play is indeed "foul", the action murder, yet Hamlet still clings to the old delusion that it's a game. The duel with Laertes is a game (IV.vii.105, V.ii.235, 266). Dispatching his school fellows to the slaughter is part of a play they have performed together (V.ii.30–1). Actions that a man might *play*? Actions that a *man* might play? Macabre but appropriate, in the end the corpses are set high on "a stage" for public view. The play's the thing.

The Claudian world is a globe distracted by its deceptions. Hamlet is a player distracted by his vision of the globe, its

57

image inside his own head. Even he is caught in the world's deceit. Between the mind which reasons and the body which acts there is a gulf not unlike the division of thought from action in Claudius's seeming. The gulf between conscience and action is Hamlet's version of the world's seeming. It is what puts him alone with his labour. Action of any sort becomes by this metaphor a matter of role-playing. And Hamlet finds the same inhibitions against playing the revenger as he does against any form of play-acting.

In a world of seeming and acting men are alone with their thoughts. Most isolated are the protagonist and antagonist, the chief actors, the arch deceivers. Their game, the fencing between Claudius and Hamlet which runs from Act 2 till the end, is one that only two can play. Allies are casually slaughtered.

> 'Tis dangerous when the baser nature comes
> Between the pass and fell incensed points
> Of might opposites.
>
> (V.ii.60–62)

A duel it is, between two men isolated by their very involvement in their interplay. Their isolation is cause and effect of their deceptions.

Claudius, as king and a clever man among innocents, is isolated by the secret crime he committed to make himself king. But Hamlet has no such reason for his isolation. He is not alienated just for being a student in a court of hard drinkers or a genuine mourner amongst shallow emotions. It is not youth, melancholy or grief that isolates him. Hamlet is quicker in words, wit and (in the end) swordplay than any of his peers, but although these qualities might set him above his fellows they would not necessarily set him apart. And from his first appearance he clearly is apart, when he enters, a reluctant last in the ceremonial opening procession of the king in council. Placed by birth at the centre of affairs in the Claudian world, his sympathies are with the soldiers and Horatio on the periphery, out in the cold of the moral battlements. Conscience sets him apart, first in his condemnation of the venial world

58

of shallow feeling and easy seeming, later in his assumption of the role of dustman to the moral grime.

Hamlet could have done what Laertes did and assault the throne with mob violence. Claudius acknowledges his popularity with the people while admitting their readiness to believe ill of himself. Horatio and Marcellus were at his elbow to give assistance if need be. But like Witoldus of Lithuania Hamlet holds it right to taint only the individual most centrally concerned with the bloody task of revenge murder. His choice of solitude, like his grief, is a more positive act than the traditional picture of a weak, indecisive and unsoldierly heir to the throne usually allows. Thus conscience can make individuals of us all.

Lack of resolution may have been Hamlet's own accusation against himself, but it is not by any means the view of other characters in the play. Claudius, who handles the other lordlings of the younger generation with contemptuous ease, consistently treats Hamlet as a deadly danger. Gertrude may fondly say he's fat and short of breath once he has beaten Laertes twice running at the foils, but she speaks it out of possessive pride. Ophelia may be more than a little biassed and inclined to over-estimate her loss when she weeps for the overthrow of her noble lover's mind, but she believes what she says when she proclaims him the perfect gentleman, the complete allrounder, "The courtier's, soldier's, scholar's eye, tongue, sword." Much more to the point, in his actions in the play he demonstrates all the qualities she ascribes to him in full. In his judgement of beauty (between father and uncle), in his learning and his wit, even his rather presumptuous lecture to the actors on how they should not mouth their speeches (though in the event it turns out they need it); in his concern for honesty, in the honour which makes him take arms against Claudius and in the prowess which faces the pirates and defeats Laertes, at every turn he is 'our Sidney, our complete man'. He does not quote Montaigne in his soliloquies just for effect, nor dwell on the faculty of reason as the highest of attributes just because he is aware how little Denmark prizes it. He does not need Fortinbras's patronising last words to endorse his soldierly potential.[2]

Hamlet does not lack loyal friends, however easily Claudius manoeuvred the election against him. Marcellus and the sentries on the battlements could have gone to Claudius with their story, but choose instead to approach Horatio as the man who could judge their story and take it to Hamlet. Horatio is a curious piece of plot mechanism, close to the throne when Ophelia is mad and yet a stranger to Laertes and Osric; a newcomer to Elsinore and yet informed about the preparations for war. He is himself such a solitary that hearing of letters to him he can think of nobody who might write to him except Hamlet (IV.vi.4-5). A mirror to Hamlet, he listens to all his news and plots, is (belatedly) the only recipient of Hamlet's confidence about the ghost's story, spies for him during the Mousetrap, and tells the whole sad tale for him at the end. Loyalty could ask no more than he offers. And yet Hamlet keeps him at a distance from events, at first dismissively, later as the passive mirror to Hamlet's active part. The antic disposition and the gulf between Hamlet's new learning and the book-learning of "your *philosophy*" hold them separate until Hamlet can bring himself to tell Horatio the ghost's story. Horatio is not on hand when the consequences of Polonius's death are being sorted out by Claudius. He has no part in Hamlet's adventures on the voyage to England. Hamlet is indeed "dreadfully attended", as he tells his other shadows, Rosencrantz and Guildenstern at II.ii.264, alone and haunted by a dread image and a dreadful labour.

Melancholy adust and thoughts of suicide are integral to such a situation. Hamlet thinks wistfully of suicide in soliloquy at I.ii.132 and III.i.76. He does not set his life at a pin's fee (I.iv.65), and would happily part with it (II.ii.216) to step into his grave (207). The antic disposition, disguise though it is, also serves as an outlet for his unconcealable antipathy to life on earth under the Claudian regime. Like the traditional 'antics' of the Elizabethan stage he clowns, mixing elation with misery, manic and depressive by turns. Blow following blow, the world-weariness of grief and disgust, the monstrous burden of revenge, the loss of all hope for anything besides revenge and death, each one confirms his solitariness. Like an Alceste, that other archetypal misanthrope, he loathes the way of the world, but unlike Alceste he can't sit back nursing his revulsion: he has a job to do. He has been chosen, is unique, apart. He bears the world's sorrow and the Augean labour of Hercules.

CHAPTER 4

HAMLET'S GLOBE
(2) : SCOURGE AND MINISTER

The gravedigger started his work the day young Hamlet was born. Thirty years on our hero, at the height of his powers, courtly, scholarly, soldier-like, heir apparent at the next election, takes eight members of the Danish court with him into the house the gravedigger has been preparing for him. Blood and judgement curiously commingle in this disposal of the innocent and the guilty together on the stage of the distracted Globe.

To see justice in the execution of revenge at the end of *Hamlet* calls for either gross oversimplification or a radical redefinition of the concept of justice. The innocent are dead too. Ophelia did nothing to deserve in any ordinary sense of the word her madness and suicide. Even Gertrude, lecherous and possibly adulterous though she was, guided by blood more than judgement, paid heavily for faults which would usually be considered venial as much as venal. But the chief pathos, pity for an unjust death, is usually reserved for Hamlet himself, the only corpse selected for note by living Fortinbras in the finale, protagonist, hero, virtuous punisher, God's scourge and minister. Although at least five times a murderer by the time he dies (Polonius, Rosencrantz, Guildenstern, Laertes, Claudius and to some extent Ophelia), he is the antithesis of the criminal. So what is the nature of justice in the play?

Hamlet, uniquely among Shakespeare's tragic heroes, cannot be held responsible for the tragic situation he finds himself in at the outset. Lear, Othello, Macbeth, Antony initiate their own disasters, but in this play Claudius alone is responsible. Hamlet lives through three Acts, half the play, before he can be said to do any wrong. He himself, at the moment of his first murder, seems ambivalent about his guilt. With Polonius freshly dead at his feet he tells his mother

62

> heaven hath pleased it so,
> To punish me with this [i.e. the corpse], and this with me,
> That I must be their scourge and minister.

(III.iv.176)

Hamlet has punished Polonius for his spying and is punished himself by being provoked into the crime of murder. That much is unambiguous. Hamlet is both executioner and victim of dead Polonius, and heaven has chosen to give him that dual role in order that he might be both the scourge and the minister of God. Only now is his destiny clear, and even now he voices it in the ambiguous expression of the figure of twynnes.

To be a scourge and a minister of God was to be two quite different things. God's ministry was a blameless occupation, administering justice, following the commands of God's will knowingly, obediently and virtuously. Angels and ministers of heavenly grace are what Hamlet invokes for protection when he first sees the ghost. The scourge of God, however, *flagellum Dei*, prophesied by Isaiah, was a title first awarded to Attila the Hun.[1] On the Elizabethan stage Marlowe's atheist Tamburlaine claimed it for himself in his defiance of all earthly authority. God's scourge was His instrument, not His agent, his beadle's whip, used for punishing wrongdoers and due itself when in human form for ultimate damnation. To be God's scourge and minister is to be instrument and agent, criminal and innocent, damned and virtuous at the same time.

Such a hendiadys is a vision of justice which denies the easy simplicity of Albany's attempt to round off things in *King Lear*:

> All friends shall taste
> The wages of their virtue, and all foes
> The cup of their deservings.

(V.iii.302–4)

Albany's attitude in that play is the same as Laertes, exclaiming when wounded with his own poisoned sword "I am justly killed with mine own treachery", and saying of Claudius "He is justly served;/It is a poison tempered by himself" (V.ii.288 and 309–10). Tragic justice, justice in tragedies, is usually a more complex process than that. It is certainly not the easy law of making the punishment fit the crime which we sometimes mean by the term poetic justice. This eye-for-an-eye, measure for measure kind of justice simply does not happen in Shakespearean tragedies. Albany tries to administer it in *King Lear* only to be halted by Lear's inescapable "And my poor fool is hanged", an injustice for which there can be no reparation.[2] *Hamlet* differs from the other tragedies in the clarity of the hero's position. He commits no early error, has no moral flaw to make him a tragic protagonist responsible for the collapse of his universe. He is an innocent caught in the machinery of a situation engineered solely by Claudius. He is witness to a crime, and is ordered by a figure returned from the dead to avenge it. The ghost makes no mention of justice or of God's will except to reserve it for the punishment of the murderer's accomplice, Gertrude. Hamlet's death comes as the last stop on his journey to do the ghost's bidding. Is it the inevitable, proper, even the just consequence of his actions? Is it the granting of his own death wish? The death which follows his act of vengeance is not an act of justice in any normative sense of the term, earthly or heavenly.

Justice of course is more tangible when it operates through earthly law than divine law, and in most of the play it exists solely on the earthly level. The ghost reproves Hamlet in III.iv. for punishing Gertrude in defiance of his order to leave her to heaven's justice. Only Claudius when most racked by his guilt assumes that the heavens will judge and punish him, doing themselves what can't be done on earth. In the Claudian globe earthly justice can easily be perverted with a bribe. Claudius gives yet another twist to the word Hamlet berates himself with, action, when he uses it of heaven's justice. In law judgement is bound up with the legal "action" of redress. So it is too in the heavenly globe.

> In the corrupted currents of this world
> Offence's gilded hand may shove by justice,
> And oft 'tis seen the wicked prize itself

Buys out the law. But 'tis not so above;
There is no shuffling — there the action lies
In his true nature . . .

(III.iii.57−62)

Claudius is rightly contemptuous of earthly justice. He utilises
it to good effect with Laertes, first in putting his involvement
in Polonius's murder to arbitration, then in turning the executioner's "great axe" on Hamlet. Guildenstern and Rosencrantz, elaborately excusing themselves for putting loyalty to
their king before loyalty to their friend (III.iii, 8−24) are
living illustrations of how offence's hand, covered in gold/gilt/
guilt, can set justice aside. Despite the evidence of the Mousetrap, the revelation which perhaps makes Rosencrantz and
Guildenstern so self-consciously pompous in declaring their
loyalty, no courtier hesitates to help Claudius in his designs.
Justice is not a deep principle in a court habituated to the art
of words and dissembling.

Justice is not natural to a 'distracted' globe. Claudius uses
that very word of Hamlet's in a magnificently two-edged
ambiguity when he excuses his failure to set the law on Hamlet
for killing Polonius, at IV.iii.4−8:

He's loved of the distracted multitude,
Who like not in their judgement but their eyes;
And where 'tis so, th' offender's scourge is weighed,
But never the offence.

Distraction inhibits judgement and causes the wrong thing to
be weighed in the scales of justice. The ambiguity of "th'
offender's scourge" (that which scourges the offender, i.e.
the instrument of the law, Claudius the king; and that which
scourges the offender Claudius, i.e. Hamlet, scourge and
minister) points both back to Hamlet's crime in killing Polonius
and forward to his dispatch of Claudius. The globe's distraction
inhibits earthly justice and leaves it to the individual scourge.

Two words besides "action" carry legal connotations which
make themselves heard at times in the play. The ghost has a
"cause", meaning a good case in law, at III.iv.127. The word

sounds first in the play innocuously enough at II.ii.49, when Polonius tells Claudius he knows "the very cause" of Hamlet's distraction. At the end of the same long scene it resounds more weightily in Hamlet's soliloquy, "my cause" (II.ii.542), and more neutrally again shortly after when Rosencrantz reports to Claudius that his spying has not found "what cause" there is for Hamlet's lunacy. Hamlet dwells on it three times in his fourth soliloquy, after he has committed his first crime by killing Polonius, and again at the very end when dying he begs Horatio to "report me and my cause aright / To the unsatisfied" (V.ii.321−2). The other word with a strong legal connotation is "judgement", embracing both conscience and justice. Hamlet, chief sufferer from Claudius's crime, has a just cause, a quasi-legal "action" against him, calling for a judgement. Justice must be seen to be done. Horatio must "report ... my cause aright." If the lawgiver-king is not available to give judgement, justice and the law must lie in the hands of the individual conscience. Outside the normal processes of law only God's scourge and minister will perform the acts of justice in this world. Conscience unites with blood in such an "action".

Justice, however, even to a Wittenberg-trained Lutheran basing his theology on justification by faith alone, which in some respects Hamlet is, does not offer a course conscience can lightly undertake. When Hamlet appeals to the balanced judgement of Horatio to authorise his revenge as "perfect conscience" he has by then the crime of Polonius's murder on his mind. That crime shifted the onus of judgement from the judge at law to God's scourge and minister, from the regular legal process to the individual conscience. Not until Polonius is dead does Hamlet fully commit himself to his labour and define his role as scourge and minister. The problem of the virtuous man committing the crime of revenge is solved by taking away his virtue. That is Hamlet's punishment on earth, given him through Polonius's death.

The great wordsmith uses one other macabre little word to describe Hamlet's labour, nicely trapping the heavenly and the earthly implications of revenge together. "Purgation" was a term with several uses in Elizabethan times. In his notes on tragedy Aristotle used *catharsis* variously, as medicinal purging of an audience's bowels of compassion, and as a purification of the hero not unlike the Christian purgation of the soul. Elizabethan uses were even more various. It could be merely laxative ("a purgacyon . . . rubarbe of repentaunce", wrote Skelton in *Magnificence*, possibly thinking of Aristotelean *catharsis*), or it could be a purging of the hot humour by bloodletting. At the judicial level one purged one's crimes by receiving punishment and at the religious level one purged one's soul of sin by penitence, as Hamlet thinks Claudius is doing in the prayer scene (III.iii.85). Hamlet has all these applications of the word in his mind when he uses it at III.ii. 287. The Mousetrap has snapped on Claudius and he has fled. Guildenstern returns from attending him with the complaint that Hamlet's actions have left the king "marvellous distempered", not, as Hamlet naughtily suggests, with alcohol but with anger, the hot and dry choleric humour for which purgation by bloodletting was the standard treatment. In such a case Guildenstern should send for Claudius's doctor, says Hamlet, "for, for me to put him to his purgation would perhaps plunge him into far more choler." Bloodletting would no doubt purge Claudius's crime on earth and his soul in heaven. But with Hamlet as doctor the heat of damnation would be the more likely result – far more "choler" – than the warmth of heaven's embrace.

Letting blood was the labour of God's scourge (*Philaster*, IV.i.23–6, has a speech about a "physical Justice", i.e. a physician-judge, letting the blood of a criminal with a dog-whip). Hamlet's well-chosen word to Guildenstern pinpoints his labour as something more properly for divine than for earthly justice.

Justice is a moral question. As such it is possible to import examples from outside the play to lay alongside some of the strands in its complex weave of question and motives. Montaigne conducted an explicit discussion of the moral issues which the play touches on. There is, however, no such close and obvious parallel discussion of the psychological elements in Hamlet's situation. Consequently we run more than a slight risk of clarifying the moral at the expense of the psychological, isolating it when it should remain inextricably intermeshed with the psychological. Hamlet's torment is the inseparable combination of blood with judgement. The two together are what make his conscience.

Words and actions go a long way towards explaining the state of Hamlet's mind, and strictly they are the only evidence the play offers. The difficulty is that words and actions are the end-products of a state of mind or a series of mental states largely shaped by the basic mental outlook, the cultural, emotional and intellectual training of the individual. To trace the shape of Hamlet's mentality from its outward consequences in his words and actions back to the causes in his emotions and intellect is the main challenge to the play's reader. It is the crux of the story, the key to the play's fame, and because going back so far behind words and actions is largely speculative, it is the chief cause of the critical debate.

Partly perhaps because so many studious critics have felt a mental kinship with student Hamlet, less of the debate than one could wish has fitted the evidence of words and action in the play. Coleridge's despairing dreamer Hamlet, as he admitted, was in part the invention of that unhappy would-be dragoon. Schlegel's pale and ineffectual thinker to whom all action is repugnant and the 'romantic' critics who followed him took as their basic assumption that all Hamlet's troubles started with his melancholia. He was unfitted by nature, by the cast of his mind, according to this view, for a soldier's life or for bloody work of any kind, a recluse, an eternal student. His triumph is to subdue his nature, suppress his natural squeamishness and fulfill his repellant task even though, a born procrastinator, he waits until the last possible moment to do it. The triumph is internal, almost one of endurance, outstaying his natural indolence, rather than a victory against any of the difficulties in the outside world.

Much of the play supports this view. At the outset Hamlet is acutely depressed, anxious to leave the court and return to his studies at Wittenberg. These circumstances are set out before the ghost turns the action into a revenge drama, and obviously they are one major cause of the difficulty Hamlet has in facing up to the labour of vengeance. He takes his time even before putting the truth of the ghost's word to the test with his Mousetrap. And he does die at the end "like a soldier", successful, composed in his mind, after what certainly is the most long drawn-out process of revenge-taking in Elizabethan, Senecan or any other drama. But it is not a suspense plot. The interim between Hamlet learning his task and executing it is packed with matter more substantial than the sight of Hamlet dithering while his audience waits in suspense to see when he will finally make up his mind.

The body of the play is a story of continuing mental conflict, certainly. But the conflict is a debate, a display of questions and answers, questions without answers, doubts and hesitations some of which are no more than hinted at. There are reasons for Hamlet's delay, not emotional hang-ups alone. Emotion and morality, blood and judgement interact in Hamlet's mind to produce his mental state. Like Montaigne and the Donne of the new philosophy which calls *all* in doubt Hamlet has struggled to the very frontiers of contemporary thought, is lost in a no man's land of contingencies and doubt. It takes a strong mind, not a weak one, to make that journey.

The book Hamlet reads is Montaigne, the essayist who lived in a lonely tower through ferocious religious wars, whose creed was "philosopher c'est douter", to think is to question. The sound of Montaigne is in all Hamlet's soliloquies, most strongly when he muses on suicide. *Esse aut non esse*, to be or not to be, the decision whether life is worth living, is the basic question of Montaigne's philosophy.[3] Death (in Florio's English translation of Montaigne) is "a consummation of one's being . . . a quiet rest and gentle sleep, and without dreams." Hamlet glosses Montaigne in his third soliloquy (III.i.56–82) and has him in mind in all his musings on death in Act 5. To think is to doubt; there's nothing good or bad but thinking makes it so. In a world of uncertainties death is the only organising principle for human conduct. It concentrates the mind wonderfully, and more to the point it is the time, the

69

only time, for judgement of how well a man has lived his life. "Philosopher c'est apprendre mourir." Death is the basis of judgement in human ethics.

Hamlet of course is not tucked away in Montaigne's ivory tower. He has a job to do in a political world where he needs the courage of a soldier and the cunning of a spy. Death will come, but the process of learning how to die in conditions of such stress is enormously complex. Having been taught to doubt, he has no familiar tradition or code of conduct to guide him. He has to find his own path, testing the way at every step. He is at the frontier of human thought.

Amongst the historically accurate details of tenth-century Denmark preserved in the play — elective kingship, the English vassalage, the castle at Elsinore — there is one outstanding anachronism. Frederick the Wise of Saxony founded the university of Wittenberg at the beginning of the sixteenth century. Small though it was in the first century of its life, it grew to fame easily, first through its professor of Biblical Theology, Luther, and secondly by its place in the story of Faust, a myth firmly anchored in the religious controversies of Lutheran Germany. To place Hamlet at university there was to introduce a deliberate and conspicuous anachronism. More than that, it emphasised Hamlet's alienation from the thoroughly secular and unacademic court of his home, and most important of all it indicated a gulf much wider than that of soldier from student between young Hamlet and his father.

Old Hamlet was a warrior prince, forbidding in manner, military in his interests. His victory over old Fortinbras was in single combat to decide a territorial dispute. On the battlements he appears in armour carrying his field marshal's baton (the "truncheon" of I.ii.202), marching with "martial stalk" and frowning as in battle. A figure for Hamlet to admire: "so excellent a king," a Hyperion compared with the satyr Claudius (King Hamlet himself calls his brother "a wretch, whose natural gifts were poor / To those of mine", I.v.51−2). And yet of course Hamlet's admiration is from a distance. Hamlet knows he is not built in the Herculean mould of "monarchs and outstretched heroes" (II.ii.258−9). The difference moreover

70

is more than a matter of physique and disposition, a preference for books over battles. No student went innocently to Wittenberg. Hamlet has a Lutheran, almost Puritan cast of mind, reformist, sensitive to his conscience, hostile to deep drinking, gaudy clothes, lechery, dishonesty. His father on the other hand is in the traditional mould, and has strong affinities with the old doctrine. Honourable and virtuous as he was ("whose love was of that dignity / That it went hand in hand even with the vow / I made to her in marriage", I.v.48−50), he feels the pain of death as excruciating because of his loss of absolution, the Extreme Unction of the Catholic Church.

> Cut off even in the blossoms of my sin,
> Unhouseled, disappointed, unaneled;
> No reckoning made, but sent to my account
> With all my imperfections on my head.

$$(I.v.76−79)$$

Luther in denying the Catholic doctrine of the *opus operatum*, God's hand working in the seven sacraments, had gone a long way towards destroying the importance of the sacraments. Calvin retained only two, baptism and the Eucharist, and the English Church went along a parallel road. By 1600 in England Extreme Unction was distinctively Catholic, foreign and old-fashioned, a sacrament only for those who submerged their doubts in the Church and obeyed the priesthood as supreme authorities in their sphere. Shakespeare labels the old king conservative and young Hamlet radical in their religion. The generation gap yawns there even more than between warrior and student. When Hamlet swears by the saints he opts for Saint Patrick, patron of mistakes and confusion.

A gulf of such dimensions as these separates father and son in far more than dogma and occupation alone. Choice of dogma and occupation are outward signs of inward mental states, and inward differences show in everything. It has been quite reasonably assumed that the primary justification for including the religious gulf amongst the play's background details must be its significance as the basis for the difference between Hamlet's attitude and his father's over revenge. For old Hamlet revenge is an unquestionable duty, an automatic response of blood and honour, more Viking than Christian, appropriate to one whose conscience in such matters is safe in the keeping of the Church. For young Hamlet it is a question of "conscience" in which Christian teaching pulls him in different directions. Filial duty, love of good against bad, of Hyperions before satyrs, an occasion to take arms against the chief cause of rottenness and Hamlet's melancholy: all these combine to uphold the ghost's demand. Against it is the Christian duty to suffer fortune's slings and arrows, and the word of the Lord keeping vengeance to himself.

The background details support the view that Hamlet's moral qualms grow from the ethics of revenge. His protestant individual consciousness, his emphasis on conscience and the related balancing of "judgement" against blood, his acceptance of the title of God's scourge, even his doubt whether the ghost might not be a devil sent to tempt him, all lend support to the identification of a strong moral component in his "conscience". But his own explanation for his delay is psychological. Apart from cowardice or merely human timidity, it can only be the paralysis which comes with intense depression, "my weakness and my melancholy" (II.ii.576).

The religious constraint against revenge seems to carry little more weight with Hamlet than the political constraint against killing kings. On the one occasion when he contemplates a religious standpoint, in the beginning of the "To be or not to be" soliloquy, he almost at once discards it.

Whether 'tis nobler in the mind to suffer
The slings and arrows of outrageous fortune . . .

(III.i.56−7)

Christian patience, suffering nobly borne, is the first alternative to revenge. Suicide is the other, and the one he dwells on. It too, of course, calls for positive action and is therefore subject like revenge itself to the curse of hesitation. It is thinking about suicide which "makes cowards of us all". The choice is between passion, almost in its theological sense, and action either in suicide or revenge.

72

But it is not a choice Hamlet spends any time debating. His case as he puts it in that soliloquy is a general one, cast in general terms. The name he puts highest is not nobility but action. Thought of the kind the soliloquy illustrates is hostile to action.

> Thus conscience does make cowards of us all,
> And thus the native hue of resolution
> Is sicklied o'er with the pale cast of thought;
> And enterprises of great pitch and moment,
> With this regard, their currents turn awry,
> And lose the name of action.
>
> (III.i.83–88)

This is the conclusion which ignores the Christian constraint and advocates thoughtless action. And within the hour Hamlet has committed his thoughtless act of killing Polonius, the act that makes his course of action irrevocable.

The turning-point of the whole play is that, Hamlet's first unthinking action. To Gertrude's horrified exclamation "What hast thou done?" her son answers triumphantly "Nay, I know not." (III.iv.26–7). To the solitary man bent single-mindedly on his purpose every movement is the enemy's, and every death is a victory. What to the queen is a "rash and bloody deed" to Hamlet is something else altogether. Its bloodiness he waves aside – "Take thy fortune" he says, dismissing the corpse. Its rashness is its enabling power. Rashness, acting on impulse, is the way to his revenge. He remembers the queen's word in this context some time later when his second unthinking action has also ended in blood. In V.ii. when he tells Horatio of how he despatched Rosencrantz and Guildenstern the word prompts a digression on its usefulness.

> Rashly –
> And praised be rashness for it; let us know,
> Our indiscretion sometimes serves us well,
> When our deep plots do pall.
>
> (V.ii.7–9)

Acting on impulse works.

To choose revenge, and not to think about the means, is the implication of the third soliloquy, and a choice confirmed by Hamlet's subsequent conduct. It has been said truly enough that his conduct grows rougher and his thinking coarser as the play develops.[4] Step by step he commits himself deeper into the jungle of intrigue and murder. "Forgive me this my virtue", he sarcastically tells his mother, "For in the fatness of these pursy times / Virtue itself of vice must pardon beg" (III.iv. 154—5). Like the dyer's hand he takes on the bloody colour of his work. The labour of revenge undertaken, he accepts its dirt too. "The hand of little employment hath the daintier sense", he says of the gravedigger, his fellow-worker.

To some extent the attitude of mind he displays in the last Act confirms this choice. He has a confidence, voiced at the end of his digression on fortunate rashness, in the "divinity that shapes our ends, / Rough-hew them how we will." He has reached the end of his doubtful thinking. He will wait ("The readiness is all") for the moment when death will come. A death, his own or Claudius's, is no more than saying "one" to acknowledge a hit with the foils (V.ii.74). His grasp of the situation is prophetic.

Perhaps the most difficult point of all to argue over *Hamlet* is the view that this final position he adopts is wholly moral, a proper deduction from his circumstances as to what is the best course open to him. The case for adopting such a posture on emotional grounds is clear cut — much clearer than the moral grounds. But something is there, in this final insistence on destiny, which implies a mind settled emotionally largely because it is settled morally. And that takes us back to the point when Hamlet identifies himself as "scourge and minister" after killing Polonius.

In Act 5 Hamlet repeats his cool assertion of faith in pre-destination, the divinity which puts a final polish on the course of our lives, when he quotes *Matthew* 10 : 29, "There's a special providence in the fall of a sparrow" (V.ii.202—3). Such calm confidence in destiny is fitting in a play patterned so that the gravedigger starts his trade on the day of Hamlet's birth. But he has already made the same statement more crudely in more violent and therefore more revealing circumstances. At the end of the savage little encounter at Ophelia's grave (V.i.227–73) Hamlet ferociously parodies Laertes' ranting grief in ironic memory of his own passioning. His capacity for love is greater than Laertes' ("Forty thousand brothers / Could not, with all their quantity of love / Make up my sum") and so therefore is his passion. But grief looks into the past and there is still the awful present to deal with. Ophelia is dead and in the past. "What wilt thou do for her?" he asks Laertes. What good will grieving for the dead do when the present is such a distracting burden of grief? Grief is a self indulgence. It is not possible to be callous over Ophelia's death as it was over her father's, but the time for passioning is gone and the mood must be readiness for revenge. The current has caught everyone, has swept away Ophelia, and not even a Herculean hero can swim against it now.

> Let Hercules himself do what he may,
> The cat will mew, and dog will have his day.
>
> (V.i.272–3)

This exit line of Hamlet's is a bitterly crude version of the biblical tag from *Matthew* he uses later to Horatio. The old proverb about nobody being able to change a cat's mew is a straightforward declaration that free will has its limits. In this context it is like a dismissive shrug of the shoulders, directed at would-be Herculean Laertes, Hamlet's alter ego as man of action. Nobody can now do anything to dead Ophelia or prevent the deaths to come. The current has them all.

What has made Hamlet by now see his destiny as inevitable? Very early in the play, in his first soliloquy, he made his first comparison of himself to Hercules, the archetypal man of action, the God-like son of a god, the man who accomplished twelve inhuman labours and in the end conquered death itself. Hamlet's task is Herculean, that he knows, and knowing himself no Hercules he groans under the load. By Act 5, however, his attitude is different. Belligerent Laertes is now the Hercules figure, and clearly is less capable than Hamlet of cleaning out the Danish stables. Hamlet knows he has a better grasp of the situation than Laertes. It is not the expectation of death at the cry of "one" which has altered Hamlet's attitude to the Herculean nature of his task. That was a consummation long and devoutly wished for. What has changed in Hamlet is that now he knows he will accomplish his task. The problem of thought has been set aside. Action is a matter of readiness to act on impulse, of responding to the occasion without time for thought. That is what Polonius's death has taught him. It committed him to serve as God's scourge, destined for death himself, and minister, agent of the good. And it taught him the means. All the morality of revenge killing, and all the doubts that make him hesitate, can be ignored by acting on impulse. The readiness for murder and for death is all.

– ii –

Hamlet is as innocent of any crime as Ophelia until he kills Polonius. That rash deed is the play's turning point because it commits him irrevocably to the "action" of the Claudian world. It finally turns him criminal. The notorious misanthropy which holds him apart from the deep-drinking court, which sends him to Wittenberg rather than to Paris, has its roots in a mental condition which makes his psyche deeply moral and thoroughly exacting in its standards. Only by such standards would we think to condemn the normal human reasonableness of Claudius's conduct and his court.[5] His "pious action", his comradely drinking, Gertrude's happiness, a "most seeming virtuous" behaviour pattern in a lady who indeed sees herself doing no wrong, Polonius's loyal spying in the interests of the state, these are the venialities which Hamlet can't abide. He condemns drinking and gaudy clothes as if he were the Puritan whose nighted colour he wears. Gertrude sees no wrong but the small embarrassment of "our o'er-hasty marriage". Claudius acts resolutely and cleverly to protect the security of the state. Polonius does his duty as he sees it, keeping a check on his own son as the king keeps a check on his. Rosencrantz and Guildenstern proclaim their duty to the state's security as stronger than loyalty to an old friend ("Ne'er alone / Did the king sigh, but with a general groan" III.iii.22−3). Impeccable feelings, at the level of human conduct which admits a little disingenuity, a diplomatic piece of dissembling here and there as necessary if human beings are to rub along with one another. Flesh is weak and should not be required to suffer too much pressure.

Only Ophelia, humbly and dutifully obedient to her father as Hamlet tries to be to his, shares Hamlet's feeling for honesty. In the pitiful scene where she follows her father's instructions and returns Hamlet his "remembrances" he takes her for another dissembler, a bawd. "Are you honest?" he demands, and shortly after (perhaps seeing the arras where Polonius is concealed moving) "Where's your father?" So, assuming her to be of the Claudian school, he orders her off to a nunnery/brothel, a neat ambiguity which answers either likelihood, her trickery or her honesty.

In his next and last encounter with her, when he is wound up ready to spring the Mousetrap, he is offensively obscene in an almost absent-minded, certainly offhand, attempt to cauterise her love-wound. Bigger dramas are on stage than love's comedy. So when the king flees from Hamlet and his murder-trap Ophelia flees with him, leaving Hamlet alone with Horatio and his honesty. She removes herself as he wants her to. Then he kills her father and she retreats into madness and death, a pale shadow of Hamlet's own fate following the alternative course of suffering in place of action.

Only Hamlet with his follower Horatio recognises the higher code of conduct, the code which sees dissembling and seeming as the code of the trivial and venial. An element in his bitterness at the outset is, on the evidence of his outburst about seeming, the need to curb his honest passion and hold his tongue. To criticise the new king and his incestuous marriage, to condemn his mother for shallow lust, would be treasonable. There are limits to an absolute code of morality in the sublunary condition where man lives in society, in a distracted globe. Hence Hamlet's regret that suicide is not a way of escape. He is in an impasse where no form of conduct can satisfy his moral sense of the way man should behave. Blood and judgement may commingle, but they never provide in either the scientific or the philosophical sense a solution.

The reasonableness of the Claudian globe is crucial to an understanding of Hamlet's position. His misanthropy, the high value he puts on mankind in general ("What a piece of work is man"), the general miracle which he personally must reject ("Man delights not me"), stems from the need to bear his high moral sense alone in a dissembling court. The Claudians have no inkling of his alternative values. Even Claudius himself, though conscience-stricken over his fratricide, the sin of Cain, does not blame himself for dissembling and never thinks to add dissembling or diplomacy to the list of his crimes. Only Hamlet makes life difficult for everyone. It is easy to believe in Rosencrantz and Guildenstern's goodwill when they find "distraction" for Hamlet by offering him the most acute symbol of man's disingenuity, those professional dissemblers the players. "Heavens make our presence and our practices / Pleasant and helpful to him!" (II.ii.38–9) is Guildenstern's pious hope. "Practices", with its Machiavellian associations, the word Claudius uses (IV.vii.66 and 138) to describe the plot with Laertes' poisoned sword, is the right word, though it sounds respectable enough when it refers to the devices employed to keep a lunatic happy. That Guildenstern should use the word in this way is a measure of the distance between his view of the distracted world and Hamlet's.

Once he has killed Polonius Hamlet is in the Claudian soup, to sink or swim as he may. Only after that is he free from hesitation so that he can give his impulse reign with Claudian practices. At the end of the play, when Hamlet confronts Laertes before the duel and offers the hand of reconciliation, he ostensibly supports Claudius's pretence of peace-making. But he offers the velvet glove of courtesy, perfect dissembling, while speaking the iron truth beneath it. "This presence knows", he declares, as how could Claudius not know it, "how I am punished / With a sore distraction" (V.ii.210–12). God's punishment which has made him scourge and minister to the distracted globe has been evident since the death of Polonius.

Claudius, "this presence", started the mad trail of deaths in the first place and so is the first cause of the world's distraction. Hence "What I have done" in killing Polonius "I here proclaim was madness" (214). Whose madness? The king knows. "Was't Hamlet wrong'd Laertes? Never Hamlet." Mad Claudius has made Hamlet not himself. "Who does it then? *His* madness. If't be so, / Hamlet is of the faction that is wronged." Never were apology and accusation so neatly combined. Claudius is responsible for the world's madness.

CHAPTER 5

THE SEQUENCE OF EVENTS

First things last: the verbal, psychological and moral nuances in the play would have none of their peculiar complex intensity without their setting in the dramatic action. The sequence of events is of the first importance for reading the play with its nuances set in their proper context.

It opens with edgy and unhappy soldiers on duty on the walls of Elsinore: the relieving sentry is so on edge he challenges the man he has come to relieve instead of waiting to be challenged. Corrected, he gives the password which affirms the soldier's duty in defending the realm: "Long live the king!" With a tinge of reproach in his voice the departing sentry comments on how careful his relief has been not to come too soon. The relief for which Francisco gives much thanks is from pressures more troublesome than sentrygo.

These curt exchanges which open the play are enigmatic about the cause of the sentries' unease. But they are good men (Marcellus calls the departing Francisco "honest soldier"), and free consciences should not be troubled like this. Something different from the normal dangers a soldier faces is threatening them. So, with a bracing touch of Horatio's cool scepticism — the threat frightens soldiers but not scholars — the atmosphere is set for the ghost. The soldiers are simple and superstitious, but they have had the sense to get help from the scholarly sceptic Horatio before spreading alarm and risking ridicule by telling the news of the ghost's appearance to the world. They have watched the ghost twice before doing anything: proper caution and a sensible move. Equally sanely, Horatio cuts short their frightened conjectures about the apparition. His initial scepticism ("Tush, tush, 'twill not appear") is important not to emphasise its credibility when the ghost does appear but to justify his scanning the alternative explanations. It might be stalking the battlements as a

80

"portentous figure", an omen of trouble to come, a warning of danger ("If thou art privy to thy country's fate, / Which happily foreknowing may avoid"), or as a spirit made restless by its knowledge of buried treasure (the conventional reasons for ghosts to walk); or any other cause of restlessness ("If there be any good thing to be done, / That may to thee do ease") — provided, says Horatio, such a service may be an act of Christian virtue ("grace to me"). These possibilities he canvasses to the sentries and the ghost as the standard ideas why the ghost might walk. Another story, he says, "I have heard", is that ghosts have to return to their "confine" at cockcrow, as this one does. But when Marcellus starts embroidering the story Horatio cuts him short. "So have I heard, and do *in part* believe it". There is no need to indulge one's imagination.

Shakespeare concedes the necessity of the ghost as trigger for the plot, but having done so he characteristically explains its origin no more than the capacity of its witnesses on stage can cope with. All three of the standard Elizabethan ideas about ghosts are represented — the soldiers taking the Catholic view that it is a soul come from Purgatory, Horatio coolly sceptical about the folklorish superstitions, reluctant to commit himself to an opinion on the theological question, and Hamlet (later) making the Protestant assumption that it may be an angelic or devilish spirit but not any man's soul.[1] The views reflect the holders.

At the end of the scene Horatio proposes the next cautious and reasonable move, to tell the ghost's son in the hope that "This spirit, dumb to us, will speak to him." There is reason for caution with so many possible interpretations of its appearance. So far, very sensible. The audience, as much in the dark as Horatio and the soldiers, can accept the ghost as an "image" of the recently-dead King Hamlet. The dead king's son lives, and so presumably is the king and hence the proper target of a report about ill omens for the state. The soldiers would be doing their duty reporting to him. But we see that things are not so straightforward from the procession which opens Scene ii and from the king's first words.

81

Hamlet's discordant appearance, black and alone at the end of the procession to the council meeting, is partly explained when the king begins by saying

Though yet of Hamlet our dear *brother's* death
The memory be green . . .

Hamlet is in black for his father; his uncle is on the throne. We might wonder, if we had time, why Horatio and the soldiers should prefer to tell their secret to young Hamlet and keep it from the king. Naturally cautious and perhaps instinctively suspicious that something is rotten in the state, Horatio and Marcellus interpret their public duty in their own private way. The point is not underlined — nothing in *Hamlet* is — but it is registered twice in ways wholly characteristic of Shakespeare.

The first point develops from the curious carpentry image which Claudius uses to make a little joke in his speech from the throne. Sitting in his canopied chair, the "state" which was probably the most-used piece of property in the Elizabethan theatre, he pats it wryly as he describes the threat of invasion.

young Fortinbras
Holding a weak supposal of our worth,
Or thinking by our late dear brother's death
Our state to be disjoint and out of frame . . .

(I.ii.17–20)

This throne is not going to collapse under him. His "state" is secured by carpentry in timber which may be dead but which is not rotten. Later in the play Rosencrantz and Guildenstern use the same image more clumsily to describe majesty as a wheel with appendages "mortised and adjoined" to it (III.iii. 20). Hamlet by contrast sees Denmark as a state more properly described in an organic image, as an unweeded garden, an image supported by the ghost's revelation that he was killed with a poison distilled from a weed. In I.iv. Marcellus, confronted for the fourth time with the apparition of the dead king, draws carpentry and the organic image together with that famous and misread conclusion that something in Denmark's "state" is rotten. There is inward decay in the throne, the king's seat, and consequently in the nation at large. The frame may look sound but the materials are rotten.

Men afflicted with such uneasiness as Marcellus shows in I.i. and I.iv. may well see the course of their duty as less than obvious. When Horatio and the two sentries tell Hamlet their story Horatio is careful to explain that "we did think it writ down in our duty / To let *you* know of it" (I.ii.220–1). Hamlet takes the implication, since when they make their respectful farewells — "*All*. Our duty to your honour." — he corrects them: "Your loves, as mine to you." Loyalty is in question. They have chosen to approach the ghost's son rather than his brother the king with their news, and such a choice reflects love more than duty as Hamlet sees it. Things are not framed so orderly in the state as Claudius affirms them to be. The individual conscience is already seen, in these two points, to be at odds with the appearance of public order at court.

Apart from Hamlet in his conspicuous isolation, the council scene reflects none of the uneasiness seen in the "friends, scholars and soldiers" (I.v.141). Claudius deals with each item on the agenda smoothly: the transition from mourning for the old king's death to celebration of the new king's marriage, the threat from young Fortinbras and the dispatching of ambassadors to check him, Laertes' request to return to France, and lastly Hamlet's request to return to Wittenberg, the only item prompting any discord. Claudius introduces this adroitly by first proclaiming Hamlet his heir, removing his ground for discontent as the court would see it, then leading him on till he voices his continuing and therefore excessive grief over his father's death. That gives Claudius a convenient opening to reprove the young prince for childishness, "an understanding simple and unschooled", and the pretext he needs to keep Hamlet where he can be watched on the grounds that such grief must have "the cheer and comfort of our eye" (I.ii.116). Hamlet may object by indicating that he will obey his mother's sincere plea rather than his stepfather's dishonesty ("I shall in all my best obey *you*, madam"), but the king can afford to be generous ("This gentle and unforced accord of Hamlet / Sits smiling to my heart"), since he has got his way.

He can go off satisfied to his celebratory carousing, the "triumph of his pledge" to keep Hamlet under public surveillance as heir apparent.

Hamlet stays behind, no party to the celebrations, to voice his grief in his first soliloquy. It is the most specific of the soliloquies, the narrowest in scope since it deals only with his world-weariness, his passion. It has no call to action except holding his tongue. He regrets that suicide is not available as an escape, that Denmark "grows to seed" with a Claudius succeeding a Hamlet, and that human frailty should display itself so monstrously in his own mother. The speech is notable above all for its morality. Grief is compounded by disgust over bestial conduct, the triumph of blood over judgement. There is no hint of self-interest, the thwarted ambition which the situation invites and which some courtiers look to find in him. Hamlet as critic of the court is entirely free from the envy of self-interest, incapable of consolation, incapable even of looking for sympathy among others because he is alone in his judgement and so must hold his tongue.

And then as a denial of this isolation comes Horatio, the true "friend" that Hamlet immediately proclaims him, together with the two "honest soldiers" who out of their caution and fear have interpreted their duty as owing to Hamlet before Claudius. Even before the nature of the conflict has been identified the sides are instinctively drawn. Hamlet does not think to hold his tongue before Horatio and Marcellus.

But the friendship is no sooner acknowledged than it is put to the test. Suspicion mounts in Hamlet over the story of the ghost. He tests Horatio, thinking he detects a flaw in the claim that the figure's face was visible despite his armoured helmet, and asks if his beard was grey, knowing it to have been black touched with silver ("a sable silvered"), as Horatio correctly answers. With such unshaken testimony he can only wait and see, ("Till then, sit still, my soul!").

Scene iii, the Polonius family saying their farewells to Laertes, switches the mood. This is a living father and a happy son. Domestic as the scene is, though, it renews in a different shape the suspicion and the care for appearances evident at court. Laertes' chief message to his sister is that she shouldn't listen to Hamlet's vows of love "with too credent ear". Ophelia is confident enough, credent enough of Hamlet to take the warning casually and mock her solemn brother a little, turning his exhortation to virtue back on him. Not until Laertes has departed and her father renews the warning does she react seriously. Then she shows that Laertes was too untrusting, when she replies to her father's "Do you believe his tenders, as you call them?" with "I do not know, my lord, what I should think." A sensibly cautious answer, facing both ways, voicing doubt both of Hamlet's credibility and of the proper moral attitude. Polonius, however, like his son, gives her no allowance for understanding or caution, any more than he gives his trust to Hamlet's motives. Hamlet is "seeming", his vows "not of that dye which their investments show". Polonius's speech is a complicated set of puns, weaving financial images (brokers — investments — bonds) through metaphors of clothing, law and priestly vows of chastity. Out of the mixture of motives which his metaphors reflect his concern for Ophelia's valuable virtue leads him to order her to have nothing more to do with Hamlet. The king's announcement of Hamlet's status as heir apparent is having its effect. Thus love (Ophelia's name in Greek means "help"), blocked by a commonplace suspicion of human frailty, the opposite of Hamlet's over woman, is held in check and so intensifies Hamlet's isolation still further.

Scene iv opens with exchanges of words as curt and tense as those which opened the play in the same locality. Prompted by the noise of the king's carousing Hamlet takes the initiative to fill the pause while they wait for what Horatio has neutrally called the apparition. Hamlet's lecture on the "vicious mole of nature" has attracted comment for its apparent affinity with Aristotelean *hamartia*, the flaw or mistake which triggers some Greek tragedies and a great number of theories about tragedy.[2] On the face of it Hamlet is generalising, from the carousing which gives all Denmark a bad name to the general practice of destroying individual reputations on the strength of a single flaw. Such a flaw, says Hamlet, may be either inherited or acquired ("nature's livery or fortune's star"), and will overshadow all the virtues such a man may have. Whatever else may be in Hamlet's mind here he is not confining his attention to Claudius and his drinking, and is not thinking narrowly of his own case ("so *oft* it chances"). There is a hint of what is to come in his account of the "complexion, / Oft breaking down the pales and forts of reason" which anticipates the native hue of resolution being sicklied o'er by the pale cast of thought. At this point though in Hamlet's thinking reason is the good, and the "complexion" is a neurosis or excess of will taking bestial control over noble reason. Perhaps his melancholy is at the back of his mind, but as in all his lectures (he delivers eight altogether, five of them to Horatio), he is generalising with no specific thought of his own case. And the mole in his nature is not particularly vicious yet. Frailty thy name is legion. He has still to learn of the labour which will put a premium on resolution at the cost of reason.

Then the ghost comes. Horatio has described it as a "marvel" (I.ii.193), a thing beyond reason, his attitude combining credulity with caution, suspending disbelief. Hamlet's reaction to the marvel is instant horror and an automatic appeal to the ministers of God's grace for protection. Quick as ever though he immediately declares that he will take it on trust because it comes in his father's shape. Whether it comes from heaven or hell matters less than the question raised by its appearance, "such a questionable shape" (43). The question is of "thoughts beyond the reaches of our souls", unearthly evidence of unearthly existence. But speculation is idle. The ghost moves only when Hamlet asks it what he should "*do*". Consistent with its kingly shape it then beckons Hamlet aside with a gesture of "courteous action". He is separated from his companions both by this and by his freedom from their fear, a freedom granted by his world-weariness ("I do not set my life at a pin's fee"), his better calculation ("for my soul, what can it do to that, / Being a thing immortal as itself?"), and his excited curiosity. There is no cowardice here. Affirming his distance from his companions at sword-point, he submits himself to the ghost's secret.

Claudius emphasised Hamlet's childishness. Polonius called

Ophelia a baby for trusting Hamlet's young blood. The ghost likewise underlines Hamlet's youth in laying on him the burden of revenge. Hamlet listens humbly, almost mute, to a speech as verbose as Polonius lecturing Laertes, giving chapter and verse of the misdeed which has caused all Hamlet's grief and the sentries' uneasiness, as if Hamlet needed any aids to his imagining of Claudius's crime. Nor is his reaction young and thoughtless. He registers first his mother's baseness, then his uncle's hypocrisy, "That one may smile, and smile, and be a villain" (I.v.108), and finally "my word". This, his promise and watchword, ought to be "revenge". That is what the ghost intended. But Hamlet takes it as something passive, a reminder more than a promise, the ghost's parting cry "remember me!" – a word conjuring up the crime as much as it demands the punishment. Hamlet's wings have to carry him over wide seas of passion before he sweeps to his revenge.

Such knowledge brings isolation as well as passion. The "wild and whirling words" Hamlet keeps his friends off with say only that nothing is clear. There is great offence he swears to them, by Saint Patrick, patron of confusion. He will go so far as to declare the ghost honest, the rarest virtue in the Claudian world, but beyond that is mystery and more importantly silence. His own inability to hold his tongue he will circumvent with an antic disposition, a clown's disguise to avert suspicion. In a globe where honesty is the attribute of visitors from the other world and where men dissemble, dissembling is a necessary fault among the living.

> And still your fingers on your lips, I pray,
> The time is out of joint.

(I.v.188–9)

Man's god-like speech must fust in him unused. Secrecy is the new norm. Along with the royal throne, seat of earthly justice, the whole world is twisted askew. And the burden of putting it back in joint lies on the young heir to his father's nobility.

Act 2, the spying act, begins with an indication that some time has passed since Act 1. Laertes is in Paris and has been there long enough for Polonius to be dispatching money and letters to him. Ophelia has obeyed her father in refusing to see Hamlet and Hamlet has replied by giving her a sample of his antic disposition — presenting himself to her like a soul come from hell, as she puts it. Hamlet is spending his time in Claudian ways, dissembling his passion. The measure of his dissembling at this point lies in the form his antic disposition takes, which is by no means a perfectly 'antic' part. He does not speak clownish words, and his clothes betray more than the lover's distraction which Polonius assumes. Muddied and disordered stockings and an open doublet are marks of insanity; his sighs come from a circle of hell deeper than the forsaken lover's.

Polonius's suspicions do not run deep. So preoccupied with spying on his son that he forgets his own instructions to his daughter ("What, have you given him any hard words of late?"), his chief worry is the king's reaction to the thought that Ophelia has driven the heir mad. Claudius might blame Polonius. But honesty is the best policy in case things get worse.

> This must be known, which, being kept close, might move
> More grief to hide than hate to utter love.

> (II.i.117-8)

So Hamlet's exhibition of his disposition to Ophelia gains him a point.

Scene ii also marks the passage of time with the arrival of Rosencrantz and Guildenstern, summoned to sniff out the cause of Hamlet's distemper, and with the return of the ambassadors sent in I.ii. to check Fortinbras's invasion. Claudius's actions are effective. Devious, too, in ways which accord with the ghost's story, and suspicious beyond the scope even of Polonius. Claudius receives Polonius's wordy report of Hamlet's madness sceptically, showing how far out of the Claudius — Hamlet league the old man is, and justifying his precaution of summoning extra spies from Hamlet's own generation.

Hamlet's hostility to Polonius is automatic and powerful. The old counsellor is slow-witted, of the king's party, dishonest, a spy and potentially a pandar. Hamlet's most pointed ("pregnant") replies warn Polonius against the fleshmonger-bawd's act of loosing / losing his daughter in the attempt to trap the prince. Ophelia should not walk "i'th'*sun*", be prostituted to the prince, to catch him either in marriage or in his antic secret. A prospective father-in-law Polonius may have been once. Now he is a tedious would-be spy, a bawd in his service to the king and a pandar, one of the many objects of Hamlet's suspicion.

Two more such objects enter as Polonius leaves, a spying relay. Polonius hands them the baton as he ends his run ("You go to seek the Lord Hamlet; there he is." II.ii.220). Meeting his old friends from university Hamlet sparkles at once in an interchange of wit markedly different from his sour jibes at Polonius. Yet within a dozen exchanges he has sensed their errand and in the beaten way of friendship brings it into the open. He gives them the opportunity to be honest. "Were you not sent for?" (269). They can only answer yes, but their honesty is reluctant and the sparkle vanishes. Hamlet begins to act. He elaborates his earlier oblique hints about prisons, which Rosencrantz tries to interpret as frustrated ambition, into a speech parading a general misanthropy. So far he will be honest too. Stalemate.

Rosencrantz's introduction of the players at this point he intends as a distraction for the distracted prince, his favourite toys the tragedians from that unnamed city outside Denmark. Their reason for travelling to Denmark is fortuitous, or so Rosencrantz claims it to be. Fickle fashion prefers child actors to the "common players", a point Hamlet links with the new fashion for Claudius in Denmark (frailty, thy name is audience). But their presence reminds Hamlet of the dissembling which goes naturally with Claudius and of the parts that have to be played. He makes the point to his schoolfellows, that his welcome to the players must "show fairly outward" (355), perhaps seeming more effusive than the welcome he has offered the two spies. So he goes on to act the part of the welcoming host to the players. This he does with exemplary courtesy, greeting each one personally, reminiscing warmly, demanding "a taste of your quality" (409), unlike Polonius who clearly prefers comedians to tragedians.

89

The speech displaying the player's quality is not of course casually chosen, nor Hamlet's welcome without an underlying purpose. Rugged Pyrrhus's analogy with young revenging Hamlet, the contrast of grieving Troy with carousing Denmark, shows how little escape the distracting players really offer Hamlet. The speech, as he knew it would, spurs his dull revenge. It is, of course, only playing at murder, this *Murder of Gonzago* he now commissions from the Player, but it is as much as he can so far bring himself to do. It is "passionate" action, and a test for his doubts. The second soliloquy, ending the Act, makes explicit what has been performed already: that we have seen the "playing" of a passionate speech about revenge and that we will see another play, the plot to trap Claudius with the drama of Gonzago's murder. Hamlet re-enacts on his own the implications of what we have seen him use the players' visit for. He puts into words the thoughts he has held back while offering the Player his dissembling courtesies. His acting is beginning to move along Claudian lines. Not, however, in real action. Prompted though he is like a slow actor by heaven and hell, judgement and blood alike, he still defines his problem as being able to *say* nothing.

This is a point of transition, for all that. Frustrated by the Player's freedom to voice his "passion", once alone he tries his own passioning and finds it ridiculous. So he progresses to action of a kind: only the Player's kind, the play-acting which will force the truth out from under Claudius's dissembling, but one sort of action nonetheless. Truth still matters more at this point than revenge; judgement is more than blood.

For the first two Acts there have been spyings and suspicions but few certainties. Hamlet, moving crabwise around the question of what he should do, can "act" only in the theatrical sense, in disguise. In Act 3 comes the climax, the summation of the first movement of the play, when Hamlet murders Claudius's surrogate and makes his progress to the catastrophe of Act 5 irrevocable.

The pace of events accelerates through Act 3, and from the start some certainties begin to emerge from the clouds of suspicion. Gertrude makes it clear (III.i.38−42) that Polonius was wrong in doubting the likelihood of Ophelia marrying anyone as exalted as Hamlet. More centrally, and ironically soon after Hamlet's elaborate plan to test Claudius, the man himself admits to the audience the truth of the ghost's word (50−54). With our own doubts beginning to clear, and witnessing Claudius pressing forward with Polonius in more "lawful espials", we now meet Hamlet back in his doubting frame of mind in the third soliloquy.

Esse aut non esse is at the same time the most fundamental of questions in moral philosophy and the blankest expression of the practical problem of making any kind of choice. What is it that has the choice of being or not being? Is Hamlet contemplating suicide again, or revenge, or both? Is he debating the morality of killing the king or the stumbling blocks which "conscience" lays in the road of "action"? Is the latter a generalised expression of the former? All of these readings and more have been canvassed. There is a lot to be said for Harry Levin's view[3] that the soliloquy proceeds through a series of alternatives, each choice opening up another choice and in the end turning back to the original choice, to be and suffer or not to be, in oblivion. But if the argument does progress as dialectically as this, I think, it should be more obvious. It seems to move rather randomly, as a series of associated thoughts, each separate idea adding to the complexity of the question expressed at the outset and offering no ready way to an answer.

The question is one of conduct (whether 'tis *nobler* to take one course or the other). Characteristically Hamlet voices it in general terms, not as a problem uniquely his. The labour of revenge is hardly a *sea* of troubles. The proud man's contumely, the pangs of love despised or undervalued, the insolence of office are not his burdens. Conscience makes cowards of us *all*, if we are thinking creatures. Isolated though he feels himself to be in Denmark, Hamlet does not feel that his problem is unique. Equally characteristically he expresses the problem in terms of his favourite "twynnes". To be is to suffer, in passion; not to be is to die in suicide or action.

"Conscience" stands with passion against "resolution" and action; judgement is alternative to blood, reason what stands against the actions of the beasts that lack discourse of reason. But not to act is to be a coward. This is what he had reproved himself for in the second soliloquy little more than a hundred lines before ("it cannot be / But I am pigeon-livered," II.ii. 551). Now he muses less self-tormentingly. He is on the horns of a choice basic to human nature poised as it is between bestial oblivion and angelic reason. It is a gordian knot only to be cut with the sword that kills Polonius, the unthinking impulse that makes Hamlet criminal.

But first comes the fair Ophelia, another honest creature painfully struggling to obey her father. Hamlet at first receives her almost abstractedly. He has scared her off, has said "Adieu" in his letter. She should not be in this business any more. She soon needles him, though, because her charge is of all things that he is fickle. The sweet perfume of his words which accompanied his gifts are worthless. And the words are lost because Hamlet has become "unkind" (III.i.98−102). It is a modest but firm reproof to Hamlet for his behaviour, a desperately innocent attempt to act properly, as if the prince she confronts were not dangerously lunatic. But it takes two to act properly. His reply when she hands back the gifts is mocking incredulity − "Ha, ha! Are you honest?" To him she is more than anything else a pawn in the dissembling world of Polonius and therefore no intimate of the solitary revenger. There must be more to giving up these gifts than appears on the surface. He now treats her with the hostility previously aimed at her father, while (as with his half-warning letter at II.ii.109−124) he urges her to escape from such a world. When she then attempts to invade his isolation by praying for him it drives him to distraction and he rejects her first generally − ranking her with women in general, those who jig like Polonius − and then specifically by declaring there must be no more marriages, least of all his to her. It is the behaviour of women which "hath made me mad". Jigs, wanton both in frivolity and in their hint of sex, are the essence of the corrupt world of dissembling. Presenter himself of the ostensibly frivolous

Mousetrap, Hamlet later scornfully characterises himself to Ophelia as "your only jig-maker" (III.ii.117).

Hamlet rushes offstage after berating Ophelia, perhaps unable to bear her tears. His parting advice is savagely ambiguous, to escape from the dissembling, jigging world to the honesty either of a nunnery or a brothel, amongst Venus' nuns. Ophelia's response is entirely honest. She is distraught, incapable of even beginning to understand Hamlet and concluding inevitably that he is truly insane, "blasted with ecstasy", the passion which takes a man out of his proper self, his "noble mind". Claudius and Polonius, entering while she weeps and ignoring her totally, speak in total contrast, their businesslike words counterpointed by her weeping, about what their spying has found. The king now openly declares Hamlet to be dangerous and with his usual promptness decides to get him away from the court. The time for spying has gone, so Claudius moves into action. But Polonius is slower and wants more spying, hopeful perhaps of getting final confirmation of his theory that Hamlet is mad for love of his daughter.

Scene ii starts with Hamlet as presenter of his court entertainment, rehearsing his players, teaching the professionals their job, advocating (with some irony in view of his speeches to Ophelia) the use of "temperance" in speech and action. Hamlet's taste is for tragedy, and he urges them to avoid the clowning (including jigging) which comedians provide for Polonian tastes. The show, the Mousetrap which is to catch Claudius with words, "trapically", must go off properly.

Hamlet is not taking his plan lightly in any way. Apart from doctoring the text – all the speeches of the players are pointedly relevant to Denmark and any of them might be Hamlet's "dozen or sixteen lines" (II.ii.514) – he has to guarantee the king's attendance, dispose his audience conveniently, and above all explain the ghost's story and his plan to Horatio. This he has done, along with preparing the playtext, by now ("the circumstance, / Which I have told thee, of my father's death" 72–3). Telling Horatio of course marks a shift away from the policy of silence, a breach in the veil

93

of isolation and suspicion Hamlet wrapped around himself at the end of the first Act. He too is beginning to move towards action. Horatio is now his co-conspirator, assistant in the plan to trap Claudius, though still only as witness to the truth, not actor. Understandably sentimental for a moment now his isolation has ended, Hamlet praises Horatio for his temperate balance of blood and judgement, that reasoning judiciousness which must join with Hamlet's in assessing Claudius's dissembling.

> after, we will both our judgements join
> In censure of his seeming.
>
> (82–3).

Wryly Horatio compares his job to watching a cutpurse, an image of Claudius as a thief in the crowd at a play which Hamlet no doubt appreciates since he uses it later to Gertrude (III.iv.100).

Claudius enters ceremoniously as at I.ii. Hamlet speaks offensively to him, to Polonius, his mother, and to Ophelia, who has not obeyed his order to escape and is rewarded with some aggressive obscenities in the jigging vein. Hamlet is tense, on edge. He has planned, thought out, carefully prepared his "action" this time, and can hardly control himself as his resolution prepares to take the name of action.

And then the "play" begins, with the disconcerting dumb-show which leaks the whole story. Dumb-shows were old fashioned by 1600, and Hamlet suffers for having overlooked the possibility that the players might still use one. They did not usually "import the argument of the play" (130) as Ophelia conjectures, and there has been a lot of speculation both about why Shakespeare inserted this one, and more importantly why Claudius takes no notice of it.[4] Certainly he asks later, at line 220, "Have you heard the argument? Is there no offence in't?" as if he had not been attending up to that point. But he asks that question after the first eighty lines of the play have been spoken, all of them concerned with a thirty-years-married queen's assurances that she would never marry again if her first husband died. The lady promises ("doth protest") too much, says thirty-years-married Gertrude when Hamlet pointedly asks her how she is enjoying the show. Claudius has good reason to be worried about the argument of the play. His question does not mean he did not watch the dumb-show.

I think the point of the dumb-show lies in the suspense which builds up through the ponderously orotund play-speeches. At the height of the Mousetrap's action, as the player king is poisoned, Hamlet himself can't bear it any longer and bursts out with the rest of the story. If we, as audience to the play-audience, know how far the story has still to run, we can better follow Hamlet in his suspense and his impatience. The dumb-show is a slow and clumsy preface to the Mousetrap, ominous in the warning it gives of how shaky is Hamlet's control of events, and adding to the suspense by showing how ignorant even the players are of what is going on. The risk of Claudius seeing the dumb-show is the first hazard in the dangerous and tense operation. I think he doesn't see it, not on the evidence of his question about the "argument" but because of several other small points. First, Hamlet is afraid that the prologue, entering after the dumb-show, will "tell all", as if he has avoided one hazard only to find himself at risk from the next. Second, he deals fairly confidently with Claudius's enquiry about the argument, and third he fills in the rest of the story after the poisoning for Claudius's benefit as if to confirm what Claudius might otherwise not be sure of, that Hamlet knows the complete and true story of the murder of old Hamlet.

It would obviously have been disastrous if Claudius had seen the whole story of the Mousetrap, because Hamlet has plotted it carefully to mislead him. The first eighty lines on the queen's assurances of fidelity are just near enough to the core of Hamlet's grief for Claudius to think they might be the hatching of that something "O'er which his melancholy sits on brood" (III.i.164). Hamlet aids this misconception by asking Gertrude how she likes the play and when Claudius intervenes excluding him from the implied condemnation. It is for the jade (Gertrude) who has saddle sores to wince.

"Your majesty, and we that have free souls, it touches us not" (227–9). With Claudius set in this way on the wrong tack Hamlet can then start to drop his hints. It is all no more than "poison in jest". The murderer is "nephew to the king". The black raven, symbol of ill-omen like black-clad Hamlet, is bellowing (like a beast that wants discourse of reason?) for revenge. Within five more lines the poison is poured, Hamlet's target stands revealed as Claudius, not Gertrude, and Hamlet can wait no longer. Claudius thus learns two things: that Hamlet knows the truth and that he intends to take revenge. The challenge to the duel has been thrown down. Claudius staggers off, taking with him the whole court (including bemused Ophelia, who had no way of understanding the play's argument at any point), and leaving Hamlet with Horatio in possession of the stage.

From this point on the contest is in the open between the "mighty opposites". Hamlet has thrown the gauntlet down in front of Claudius. But this is not an open duel, and Hamlet lets the initiative slip. What we now witness is Hamlet frittering away his time and passion in purposeless exchanges: exultation with Horatio, contempt with his schoolfellows and Polonius, and finally acceptance of Polonius's plan to set him up for more spying in Gertrude's closet. His mood may admit more blood than judgement ("Now could I drink hot blood" 364) but his careful plotting of the Mousetrap has extended no distance beyond the test of Claudius, and he is left with passion, not action. The long climax is not yet through. Hamlet wastes time while Claudius acts, thinking blood but not clear in his mind how to enact his thoughts. The final commitment to blood is a choice still in the balance.

Scene iii opens with Claudius, quick as ever, ordering Hamlet's immediate banishment. Now fully alerted to the danger, not merely suspicious, he is impatient with Rosencrantz and Guildenstern's ponderous self-justification and curtly sends them off to deal with Hamlet before he turns to confront his conscience. Such resolute action, preceding the affliction of conscience as it does, provides the Claudian answer to the question of choice in Hamlet's third soliloquy by its schizoid separation of the self-interested action from the guilt that similar actions in the past have burdened him with. It sets the stage aptly for the crisis of choice which next confronts Hamlet when he finds the king's back opportunely turned. "And now I'll do it . . . And so am I revenged –?" Red resolution is discoloured by pale thought: "that would be scanned" (74–5). This, the only scene where Hamlet and Claudius are alone together, has a good claim to be the central scene of the play. Interposed between the Mousetrap snapping shut and Hamlet's first murder of a Claudian surrogate, it grotesquely parodies Hamlet's essential problem. Claudius is at his mercy as he stands, sword in hand, like bloody Pyrrhus over Priam. We perhaps recall the player's speech:

> For lo! his sword
> Which was declining on the milky head
> Of reverend Priam, seemed i'th'air to stick.
> So, as a painted tyrant, Pyrrhus stood
> And, like a neutral to his will and matter,
> Did nothing.

(II.ii.452–7)

This Priam, although at prayer, is hardly reverend. This Pyrrhus, black rather than the tyrant's red ("total gules"), for once is tricked by seeming. He takes the appearance of reverence, the unsuccessful attempt to repent where the words fly up but the thoughts remain amidst earthly things, for the reality and does nothing.

The scene parodies the usual realities because Claudius for once is not dissembling, but struggling honestly. Hamlet for once is less than honest with his thoughts. To exploit the apparatus of heavenly grace as he thinks he should do for the maximum punishment of his victim, to catch him full of sin, is not the only thought which might give him pause. To kill a man at prayer was a disgrace like cutting his throat in the church, the worst offence Laertes can think of. The classical precedent was there in Paris, who killed Achilles while he was praying to Apollo in the Temple of Pallas Athene. Seneca called that a shameful action in the *Troades*. Caxton's *Recuyell*,

97

which Shakespeare consulted for *Troilus and Cressida*, takes a similar attitude to it.[5] Hamlet is here commingling blood and judgement into confusion, affirming the less happy view of things set out in the third soliloquy. Hamlet arguing himself out of his bloody action is unconsciously parodying his own analysis of his problem.

The real climax, the end of the first half of the play, happens in the rush of events at the beginning of III.iv., up to the point where Polonius's corpse falls on Gertrude's floor. Hamlet uses his sword on Polonius barely thirty lines after sheathing it behind Claudius. It is the culminating moment towards which everything has been leading. Polonius was still after proof of Hamlet's love madness. When Hamlet arrives Gertrude is angry with him for upsetting Claudius, then offended by her grown-up son's insolent counter to her attempt to tell him off, then terrified by his sudden physical assault ("What wilt thou do? Thou wilt not murder me?" III.iv.22). He, intent on his scheme of speaking daggers to her, and holding her in her seat to listen to his denunciation, a captive audience, excited by the word "murder" takes no pause for thought this time. The long period of tension, from the thought of the Mousetrap through its performance, through the exchanges with Claudius's spies and the debate behind Claudius's back, finally breaks here. He makes a frontal assault on the curtain, symbol of the dissembling world of the spy hidden behind it. Not men but rats hide behind curtains, and even as he commits himself Hamlet triumphantly bids for the job of court rat-catcher, a whole ducat's-worth of labour. He cannot bring himself to thrust his sword into a man's back; he does not yet know if he can fight his enemy face to face, but rats behind curtains it is a moral duty to dispatch, and he does not wait to ponder that one.

His moral judgement on rats rather than his disgust with Polonius living dictates Hamlet's continuing callousness to his victim. Gertrude proclaims Hamlet's deed rash and bloody. Hamlet acknowledges the blood but calls Polonius rash. As stand-in for Claudius ("I took thee for thy better", Hamlet tells him) Polonius must share the punishment due to his master, and there will be no remorse for Claudius's death. This is the beginning of the Herculean labour of cleansing Denmark.

Hamlet in any case has a prior claim on his attention, his original intention of going to his mother to at last speak his mind. As in the first soliloquy where he claims that the first cause of his grief was his mother's dexterity in galloping to incest, so on confirming the ghost's story through the Mouse-trap his first impulse is to confront her with this fresh proof of her iniquity. Claudius needs no such moral reprimand; the assault on him will not be verbal; it will use daggers not speak them. The deepest irony of the scene is that Hamlet's intention of unpacking his heart in words of moral reproof should lead so smartly to the unsheathing of his sword in blood, the irrevocable step from passion to action.

Hamlet ignoring the dead body and hurling his words at the living queen is a powerful visual image of his disorientation, his distraction from normal humanity. It has made the scene central to the arguments that Hamlet's passion is oedipal, his motivation welling up from his subconscious rather than imported from any exterior framework of morality.[6] Moral priorities on their own would insist that Claudius be put ahead of Gertrude in the crime sheet. Of Hamlet's intense loathing of his mother's conduct the closet scene gives ample evidence; that it comes ahead of his desire for revenge on Claudius is equally clear. But why Hamlet should dispose his priorities in this way is less clear, and there is certainly no single causal link leading from either oedipal neurosis or moral righteousness to his behaviour towards his mother.

The view that it is yet 'another delaying tactic to avoid the bloodshed of revenge is contradicted by the coolness with which he regards the blood shed at his feet. The ghost when he appears, however, also totally ignores the corpse in urging Hamlet to get on with his revenge. Old Hamlet is solely con-cerned to speed his son to revenge and to protect the queen. Polonius is no more than the evidence that Hamlet has been lax over both matters. Father and son now both have the same perspective, the same priorities. So Hamlet anticipates the ghost's new message, labelling his conduct a lapse from grace "in time and passion" (108). He offers no excuse, no reason why his purpose, "th'important acting" of revenge, should have lost its sharp edge. The whole pattern of circumstances, the doubts and hesitations, the elaborate Mousetrap plot, Polonius's murder, are all swept aside as Hamlet admits that the first movement of the play has come in effect to nothing. This second visitation by the ghost is to launch the second movement as it had launched the first, and Hamlet is quicker to admit the delay as a fault than to explain it. He accepts the ghost's view, so action must replace passion.

But there is little to make it any easier to accept now than there was before. When the ghost comes Hamlet has battered his mother down with that ferociously eloquent denunciation (54–89), the truth of which she admits ("Thou turn'st mine eyes into my very soul" 90) as she begs him to stop. He starts again though, and again she begs him to stop ("These words, like daggers, enter in mine ears" 96), but again he attacks her. A third time she begs him to stop (102) and still he is shouting when the ghost enters. His subject is obsessive, the mood hysterical. And when the ghost has checked him and saved Gertrude from the final revelation that her husband is a fratricide as well as incestuous, still he must revert three more times to the vicious lechery she has fallen into. Gertrude, close to him in blood as she is, offers the only target for his words, and he must shoot them. This is the last fling of outraged morality, the last of his passioning, the final attempt to face his task with words. Not Polonius nor the ghost can hold him from that need.

As he cools more practical issues begin to occupy him. Gertrude's conduct is still his main concern, but now for the future not the past. "Confess yourself to heaven" (150); "Assume a virtue if you have it not" (161), he tells her; keep out of Claudius's bed, not only for your virtue but on the expedient grounds that Claudius must not unravel the truth "That I essentially am not in madness, / But mad in craft" (188–9).

Poor Gertrude, no more convinced of that than of anything, can only gape wordlessly at a situation far beyond her scope.

> . . . I have no life to breathe
> What thou hast said to me.

(199–200)

Like Ophelia she is ignorant of any wrongdoing, though unlike
Ophelia she has done it. Like Ophelia she will fall victim of her
own ignorance. The scene as a whole witnesses the peak of
Hamlet's passion launched against a target which is off-centre
just as passion itself is not quite central to a situation calling
primarily for action. Gertrude is guilty, therefore she is to be
assaulted by moral outrage. But she is not the central target,
therefore Hamlet speaks daggers but uses none. Passion, bottled
up so long, has to be released somewhere before the action can
start. Gertrude, venial, earthly, blood-bonded to Hamlet
himself, is the only possible target for the first, or passionate
movement of the play. And by the time Hamlet's passion gets
its release Polonius is dead and the first bloody step on the
road to the final action has been taken.

The mood of action is bloodymindedness, and the practical
thoughts that crowd into Hamlet's mind as the passion escapes
are of bloody plots. Claudius must be prevented from using
lechery to make Gertrude his spy again. The murder of
Polonius will speed up Hamlet's banishment ("set me packing",
212), and on the voyage to England he will have to face the
trap which is certainly laid for him there. So he will act against
the plotters with superior cunning, hunt the hunters. The end
of Act 3 prepares for a swift series of manoeuvres in Act 4.

In most of Shakespeare's plays Act 4 is the act in which
matters are reshuffled after the climax and set out for the
catastrophe. *Hamlet*'s fourth Act does this less than most.
We do see a number of minor characters (Ophelia, Rosencrantz
and Guildenstern) tidied away. We do see the consequences
of Polonius's murder on Hamlet and Claudius and more
drastically on his two children, setting up a new situation from
which the final confrontation will emerge. We hear in outline
of Hamlet's adventures on the England voyage and his escape.
But in spite of all these, largely because so much of the Act
happens in Hamlet's absence there is also a sense of time

accelerating, of events rolling on under their own momentum, of a situation now moving towards a confrontation, the duel, in ways which neither contestant can control. Act 4 begins with Claudius plotting to murder Hamlet on the England voyage (IV.i.30, iii.8–10, 39–45, 57–64), and ends with Claudius again plotting Hamlet's murder (vii.62, 162) through Laertes. This lack of control, attempts at action which don't quite come off, is like a new kind of delay, purpose thwarted not in passion but in action. It is an Act packed with manoeuvrings which make no progress.

In such a context we listen to Hamlet's last soliloquy. He speaks it out of the tangle of Claudius's England plot, confronted with resolute Fortinbras, contrasting with revengeful Laertes. For the third time he lashes himself for cowardice and resolves that his thoughts must be bloody or be nothing (IV. iv.66). His mind here differs from the attitude of the third soliloquy essentially in the personal application of his thoughts. The general question, to be or not to be, has narrowed now that action is under way. To acknowledge the problem as specific to him is Hamlet's last step before his final resolution, the frame of mind in which he can face both murder and his own death. That in an important sense is what Act 4 teaches him, so that by the end of it he is ahead of Claudius for the first time. Claudius begins and ends the Act in the same way, with dissembling plots. Hamlet learns the advantages of rashness, acting on impulse, preparing the mind rather than the sword or the cup of poison, letting events carry him on to the right moment.

The beginning of Act 4 follows directly from the end of Act 3, as Gertrude tells Claudius in the most protective way she can how Hamlet killed Polonius. However her defence of Hamlet by emphasising his "brainish apprehension" (IV.i.11) gives Claudius the opening he needs to expedite Hamlet's departure for England. Claudius sails as close to the truth as his audience will take. To Gertrude (and Hamlet) he pretends the voyage is for everyone's safety, especially his own, and to keep the prince out of the way until the fuss and perhaps the madness will have abated. He must labour his hardest to gloss

102

over the crime, he says, with the best of Claudian dissembling.

> . . . this vile deed
> We must, with all our majesty and skill,
> Both countenance and excuse.

(IV.i.30–32)

The Claudian contingent morality is now apparently being put into Hamlet's service.

Hamlet co-operates in scenes ii and iii, playing the madman, toying with the corpse like an amoral child. How helpful this is to Claudius he tells us in IV.iii.3–9, where Hamlet's popularity with "the distracted multitude" makes it necessary for Claudius to seem to be acting judiciously. Evidently Hamlet might have roused the mob, as distracted as himself, over his father's murder quite as easily as Laertes soon does over the murder of his father. But Hamlet's fight is a private duel, not a war. Twice in his brief public interview with the king Hamlet obliquely warns him to expect death, threatening yet keeping Claudius's crime secret between the two of them. And then, as if satisfied with threats, he leads the way to England and the plot which Claudius confirms is waiting for him there. The movements of men and events are swift in these scenes, yet still they continue to move crabwise around the final confrontation.

Hamlet departs after his soliloquy prompted by the sight of Fortinbras chasing his honour, that Hotspur-like ability to "find quarrel in a straw / When honour's at the stake" (IV.iv. 55–6). Is this the *nobler* form of conduct? Fortinbras offers an example "gross as earth" (46) for bloodyminded purposefulness, though one wholly free from the charge of cowardice. So Hamlet tots up his account. He has cause (justice), will (passion), strength (his soldierly capacity) and means (as with Polonius) to kill the king (45–6). It can only be cowardice masquerading as thought, or lack of thought ("bestial oblivion" 40), which holds him back from his revenge. Thought therefore must be bloody "from this time forth". He must join the distracted globe and set his scruples aside. And so, as Act 5 tells us, it comes to be.

Scene v moves more slowly after Hamlet's departure, letting the other consequences of Polonius's murder catch up. His daughter goes mad; his son returns from Paris honour-bound for revenge. Ophelia's madness and her death are the still centre of Act 4, opening a new perspective of destruction on the Fortinbras idea of "honour", displaying the truth that struggles through madness and innocence alike. Her love songs reflect back sadly on Hamlet's grim soliloquy of twenty lines before. Her conflation of love for her father and her lover, victim and murderer, expresses the tangled weave she has been innocently trapped in. The bawdy of her last two songs (IV.v.47—54, 57—64) and the hint of feared pregnancy ("I hope all will be well. We must be patient" 66), combined as it is with the Christian virtue of patient suffering, reflect her victimised status. To herself she is victim of her choice. She is the maid who chose to stay a maid, and who thus drove her lover mad and ultimately killed her own father, all for fear of being abandoned (as her family warned her) if she gave her lover her virginity. "And so I thank you for your good counsel" (68—9) she says to Claudius and Gertrude, good guides as they are to the government of lust. In her self-blame for her retained virtue she is the most poignant of the figures parallel to Hamlet. He has forsaken the virtue of Christian patience for criminal action; she did not, and is more distracted than he in consequence.

Claudius is not so shaken by Ophelia's reference to his lechery that he loses any of his control of local events. To Gertrude, reciting his list of troubles, he still stresses Hamlet's "just remove" (77) while acknowledging the risks of slander attending his order for secret burial "in hugger mugger" of Polonius's corpse. The speech prepares the way for Laertes to come bursting past Claudius's mercenaries ("my Switzers") demanding his revenge, and in its display of apparent shakiness only underlines the cool command with which he does out-face Laertes.

Laertes, as a figure whose conduct invariably contrasts with Hamlet's, here differs most obviously in the urgent directness of his pursuit of revenge for his father in the face of any qualms

104

of conscience, grace or the fear of death ("both the worlds I give to negligence" 131). The irony lies in the ease with which Claudius stops him and in his misdirected aim. Claudius is the ultimate cause of Polonius's death, indeed, but working his way through that causal chain is totally beyond Laertes' capabilities. The vaguest of rumours, based on Claudius's apparent protection of the murderer and the order to bury the corpse secretly have brought Laertes to this frontal assault on the king. Between vague suspicion and ultimate cause lie all the grounds which exonerate Claudius and redirect vengeance against Hamlet. And these middle grounds are Claudian territory, his favourite field of manoeuvre.

> That I am guiltless of your father's death,
> And am most *sensibly* in grief for it,
> It shall as level to *your* judgement 'pear
> As day does to the eye.

(IV.v.146-9)

Appearing guiltless to other men's judgement is Claudius's art in action.

Ophelia's return now with her flowers reflects on Laertes as her earlier songs reflected on Hamlet's soliloquy. She distributes them with potent insight. Laertes gets rosemary, the marriage token, for remembrance and pansies for the thoughts which counteract the blood of his revenge vows. Claudius gets fennel as a mark of the flattery and dissembling that envelops kings, and columbine for cuckoldry. Gertrude is given rue, for regret, to be worn differently from the way virginal Ophelia wears hers.

She gets through to Laertes in some degree, though there is a rejection of her values in his horrified response to insanity which can transform "Thought and affliction, passion, hell itself . . . to favour and to prettiness" (182-3). When she has gone, giving "all Christian souls" her blessing, Claudius is able to appeal to the young man's judgement, putting the apparent circumstances of the murder to the arbitration of "your wisest friends" (198). Claudius can afford the appearance of justice, confident that the "great axe" will fall "where th'offence is"

(212), on Hamlet, immediate cause of the great offence, and not on Claudius, its ultimate cause.

Laertes' judgement can easily be diverted against Hamlet, be he alive or dead. That Laertes will be the next Claudian surrogate in succession to his father is evident in the next scene, when the letter to Horatio (IV.vi.2−26) confirms that Claudius's opposite is not only still alive but back in Denmark. We are therefore equipped in advance to witness the next display of Claudius's dexterity, knowing before he does that Hamlet is still to be dealt with and that Laertes will be made the instrument. Claudius and Laertes enter having gone to arbitration over the murder and accepted its verdict for Claudius and against Hamlet (IV.vii.1−5). Claudius is going on to explain what steps he has taken "against these feats / So crimeful and so capital in nature" (7−8). His deviousness he accounts for as the need to avoid having Gertrude and the "general gender" blame him. But he is not (what Hamlet keeps calling himself) "flat and dull" in his pursuit of justice, as Laertes will soon learn. And at that point he finds that Hamlet is alive despite the England plot and already back in Denmark. Ironically Hamlet's letter saves him in the nick of time from telling Laertes of a crime which has failed. He of course is as quick as ever to recover and shape a new plot, "ripe in my device", which he does with the adroit flattery appropriate to the recipient of Ophelia's fennel.

Hamlet, says Claudius, is envious of Laertes' reputation at swordplay. This is implausible: Hamlet's reason for practising after Laertes went back to Paris was more potent than envy. How poor a picture Claudius paints here of Hamlet is re-affirmed a little later when they come to the details of their plot and Claudius notes that Hamlet is "remiss", off his guard because he lacks the natural suspicions of a Claudius; "Most generous", i.e. true to his father's nature, and "free from all contriving" (134−5). Hamlet is hardly incapable of plotting, as the Mousetrap has shown, nor, under pressure from the Claudian world, is he unsuspicious. Claudius does not want Laertes to think his task may be too difficult. Laertes however is thoroughly biddable. He even offers the contrivance of poison to make all sure before Claudius does, and has the poison ready to his hand, a truly Claudian precaution. Claudius's own contingency plan for a second supply of poison makes clear his true opinion of Laertes' worth when he proposes it as a "back or second" to the poisonous swordplay. He expects Laertes to have no easy task.

The scene and the Act end with the hard contrast between the murderous plotting and Ophelia's flowery suicide, that choice canvassed along with Christian suffering in Hamlet's third soliloquy. The flowers woven in her garland again spell out her message. Crowsfoot and daisies are emblems of virginal purity. Nettles and dead men's fingers have the sting of death in them, and the willow under which she drowned is the weeping tree. The choice of not to be, withdrawal from the Claudian world, distracted and distracting, is for the weak and innocent.

Act 5 opens, as Act 1 did, with men at work. Where the sentries of Act 1 guarded the living and feared the ghost, these men make homes for the dead, custom having given them "a property of easiness" (V.i.62). They talk, too, of Ophelia's suicide in earthly tones, their macabre comedy a refusal to take the affairs of the great seriously. "The more pity that great folk should have countenance in this world to drown or hang themselves, more than their even Christian" (23−5). Exchanges of rustic wit provide the necessary pause, a distancing from the conflict, before the final storm begins to gather. And they give a longer perspective on the pains and sufferings of ambition than anything else in the play, before the final destruction of the ambitious.

The initial murmur of catastrophe begins when Hamlet enters, and the clown begins to sing his folk song as he throws up his skulls. Its first stanza fits Hamlet to Ophelia ("In youth, when I did love, did love" 56); the second fits Hamlet's present case ("But age . . . hath shipped me intil the land, / As if I had never been" in love. 65−8). And finally, as Hamlet is reminded of his warning to Claudius about kings going on progresses through beggars' guts ("Here's a fine revolution, an we had the trick to see't" 81−2), the clown sings of death: "O, a pit of clay for to be made / For such a guest is meet"

107

(87−8). This pit of clay is being prepared for the maid, not the lover, but a grave maker who started work on such a momentous day as Hamlet's birth is likely soon to have more work. Now the action is long past anyone's control and moving unstoppably towards death. The procession following Polonius and his daughter to their graves will be a long one. There is a finely delicate irony as Hamlet stands musing over death in general, unaware that the grave at his feet is for the girl he loved and whose death he is, in the medium term, responsible for. The vision, so long famous in stage history, of a black-clad Hamlet holding up the skull of a jester and telling painted women they too must die, ought to include the grave at his feet.

When the funeral procession arrives, with its "maimèd rites" (199), Ophelia's death generates only sordid struggles among the living. Her flower messages have not been heeded. First passionate Laertes and intransigent priest, harder than the grave maker in his hostility to the great who have overruled the law, clash angrily. For the "shards, flints and pebbles" which the priest would throw on Ophelia Gertrude scatters flowers, confirming the priest in his grievance while asserting the truth. Then Hamlet clashes with Laertes in that extraordinary struggle inside the grave. An innocent grave, where men trample the flowers in dispute over the cause of death.

The struggle illustrates in unobvious ways how fully Hamlet now possesses the qualities he needs for his final task. It anticipates the terms of the duel to come by the clash with Claudius's new surrogate and the sight of Claudius behind him. As prelude to the duel Hamlet makes the challenger's announcement: "This is I, / Hamlet the Dane" (238−9). Only a challenger for the crown would name himself in such terms. "The Dane" is king of Denmark. When Laertes then clutches him by the throat with a curse − "The devil take thy soul!" − Hamlet is coolly alert to the verbal play. "Thou pray'st (prey'st) not well": invoking the devil for his revenge is going about it the wrong way. Hamlet has it right. He has exactly that courage which he three times before had doubted in himself. His power is not mere rashness ("I am not splenitive

108

and rash") like Laertes,

> Yet have I something in me dangerous,
> Which let thy wisdom fear.

(243–44)

The king has them pulled apart from one another. Hamlet then issues his next challenge, to the surrogate over the question whether Hamlet, despite all that has passed, his madness and Polonius's murder, loved Ophelia. Honesty must not deny that, in the face of what is past and to come. Hamlet is already bothered by his "wounded name" (V.ii.326). A few words parody Laertes' passion ("Nay, an thou'lt mouth, / I'll rant as well as thou") as a mark of how much deeper into understanding of the truth Hamlet is. It remains then only for the crack about Hercules (272–3), that out-stretched model for heroic Laertes, and the king's grim promise that Ophelia will have a "living" (lasting, so far still living) monument, before the stage is cleared in preparation for the finale.

V.ii. begins quietly, with narrative, as Hamlet tells Horatio what in the graveyard he had not seen as urgent, the details of his escape with the pirates, and the deaths he can now add to Polonius in his tally of the king's spies. He calls his action in spying on the spies to see their message for England rash, though he had denied that quality in himself a few lines earlier: his is not the splenitive, angry rashness of a Laertes, but the impulsiveness that killed Polonius. "Indiscretion" is his second word for it (8), a lack of decorum and honesty which brings results, and prompts the famous generalisation

> There's a divinity that shapes our ends,
> Rough-hew them how we will.

(10–11)

Here for the second time destiny comes into his consciousness (the first was his crack to Claudius about Hercules, and the dog having his day). This fortunate chance "should learn us" that divinity works through accidents, he says, as if the evidence was previously lacking. Heaven was "ordinant" (48) even to the signet ring with which he could seal the forged

109

substitute message. Hamlet is gleeful over his villainy, but at the same time uneasy. He insists on heaven's backing for his action. When Horatio says musingly and neutrally "So Guildenstern and Rosencrantz go to't", he defensively picks up the unconscious sexual innuendo — "Why, man, they did make love to this employment; / They are not near my conscience" (56—8). Like Polonius they came in the way of a sword-thrust in the duel "Of mighty opposites" (62). As with his challenge to Claudius and Laertes at the graveside Hamlet here anticipates his final confrontation with Claudius as a duel. That is the honest way to go about a revenge murder. On this fresh evidence of Claudius's villainy, "To quit him with this arm" is surely, he asks Horatio, "perfect conscience" (67—8). Worse than that, not to "quit him", make him pay, and to let him continue his evil ways is surely "to be damned" (69). Rhetorical questions by now perhaps: Horatio does not trouble to answer them. But for all his assertion of confidence in destiny, Hamlet still cannot help asking them.

There is much to make Hamlet uneasy. His catalogue of the king's crimes is now longer than ever,

He that hath killed my king, and whored my mother;
Popped in between th'election and my hopes;
Thrown out his angle for my proper life

and (crowning offence) "with such cozenage!" (64—7). The last item rankles. Hamlet is neither cousin nor cozener of the king. His plan is for open and direct confrontation, sword in hand. His challenge he has already thrown down (Here am I, Hamlet the Danish king). But his dispatch of Rosencrantz and Guildenstern was cozenage, and their deaths are perhaps nearer his conscience than he is willing to admit. Excuses he will not make, nor apology, except obliquely in his regret that he behaved·as he did to Laertes, the latest royal instrument. And Laertes has a special claim. "For, by the image of my cause, I see / The portraiture of his" (77—8). What roused Hamlet there was his show, his lack of silence, "the bravery (fine clothing) of his grief" (79). Laertes feels free to vent his passion outwardly to out-Hamlet the man whose "cause" is as just as his. Hamlet, still uncomfortable in his new role, is careful to be judicious. Rosencrantz and Guildenstern deserved what they got, Claudius deserves what he will get, but Laertes has something on his side.

Foppish but murderous Osric, spacious in the possession of land, is one of those flatterers whom Hamlet noted before as the type to pay out a hundred ducats for a miniature of the new king (II.ii.349). He is a fashionable bubble, "a kind of yeasty collection" who sings "the tune of the time" (175−6). Hamlet mocks him as he mocked Polonius, outdoing him in verbiage and burlesquing his excessive flourishing of his hat. But it is to be Osric who comperes the duel and holds the un-baited foil ready for Laertes. Hamlet shows how little impor-tance suspicion now has for him by accepting Osric only as an absurd dissembler who says "carriages" when he means "hangers" ("The phrase would be more germane to the matter if we could carry cannon by our sides. I would it might be 'hangers' till then" 150°−2). Osric goes with the lavish trappings of the duel in its appearance as just a game played for Barbary horses and French swords. Such excellent foppery reminds us of the range of resources which Hamlet is matched against, and that he is even now still inclined to think in terms of playing games.

Hamlet senses, without the need for spies, that the end is near. He has "such a kind of gain-giving (misgiving, against-giving) as would perhaps trouble a woman" (198−9). Laertes said when he wept for Ophelia that his tears were the womanly part of him, drowning the manly blaze of his desire for revenge (IV.vii.190). Hamlet has no tears of passion left. He is ready for death, has finally answered his own charge of cowardice. The divinity which guided him through the England voyage and which rules over the fall even of a sparrow has him under its control. He is God's instrument, scourge and minister, and can accept the death which such a role brings. "Let be" is his conclusion (206); leave him alone for events to take their inevitable course.

Claudius's mousetrap begins, a more purposeful play than Hamlet's. The king first makes the players shake hands, as if

111

the duel is to purge Laertes' enmity with a pretence of combat, another game. Hamlet, playing his part, offers courtesy while beneath it laying the blame squarely on the moral insanity of Claudius, initiator of the deaths and the accidents which made Hamlet shoot his arrow over the royal house and injure his brother revenger. Laertes in contrast stumbles through his reply. He cannot judge what is honourable for himself, and until a judgement is delivered by impartial arbitrators will "receive your offered love *like* love", on the assumption perhaps that Hamlet is dissembling. Hamlet continues to play the game, punning on "foil" airily enough for Laertes, already on edge, to assume huffily that Hamlet is laughing at him. Hamlet is being mock-modest, knowing he can win.

The tension mounts as Claudius sets up the contingency poison, echoing his earlier declaration that drum, trumpet and cannon, instruments of war music, should celebrate when he drinks. He is not playing a game. The first bout ends with Hamlet still playing, acting out his earlier claim that "a man's life's no more than to say 'One' " (74,262). More tension as Hamlet delays drinking the poison to play the second bout. Again he wins, and suddenly the odds on his taking the wager (Laertes now has to win nine of the next ten bouts) and even preventing Laertes from scoring at all are strong. And that is fatal. Gertrude, fondly deprecating the breathlessness of her soldierly son, anticipating victory, carouses too soon. Laertes, possibly spurred by the awful sight of the dissembling going wrong, whispers desperately to Claudius his determination to kill Hamlet this time. Claudius, half his ambition suddenly wiped out by his own contrivance, calculates the likelihood of that with curt pessimism: "I do not think't" (277).

At that moment Hamlet's sense of game takes him too far. Laertes' conscience is coming to wakefulness at last, and like Pyrrhus he too hesitates. Hamlet chooses that moment to taunt him with playing half-heartedly. "Say you so?" retorts Laertes grimly, and the third bout is on with "best violence" (280). At his best though Laertes can still only achieve a draw, and in desperation starts the next assault without warning to make sure of his bloody purpose. It is the last mark of Hamlet's

112

mastery of the "game" that he should be so quickly able, seeing his own blood and guessing the plot behind it, then to turn the tables on Laertes and give blood for blood to the mirror-image of his cause.

Laertes dying and perhaps revenged can speak his mind clearly. His conscience, alerted fully by death, tells him the plot was a "foul practice" (299) of the king. So with more acumen than he knows he cries "the king, the king's to blame" (302), and this time Hamlet does not pause. With a last, savage, pun on the "union" pearl of poison which binds husband and wife eternally in death, he applies poisoned sword and poisoned cup to Claudius, in a last ironic reversal. For Hamlet the instrument of death was always going to be the sword; fittingly for Claudius it is a poison as well.

Laertes' last speech anticipates Fortinbras's judgement of events. Claudius is "justly served" (309); Hamlet is "noble" (311); the slaughter of Polonius and his son is as blameless as Laertes' murder of Hamlet. There are no revenges except on Claudius.

Hamlet's dying concern that Horatio should live to "report me and my cause aright" has sometimes been taken as the mark of an insecurity reaching even beyond death. That is a view limited to Hamlet's mind, not the distracted globe it swims in. Honesty and truth have too long been suppressed under the Claudian regime. Hamlet has had to keep silent in the face of tyranny for too long. Now the king is dead: long live truth and honesty. A "wounded name" (326) would make the story a tale of blood alone, not judgement. There is nobility in the world ready to stand up to evil and it should be known. So Horatio's duty is, in exquisite phrase, to "Absent thee from felicity awhile / And in this harsh world draw thy breath in pain, / To tell my story." The felicity of the next world which is Horatio's due, and perhaps Hamlet's too, is still to come; in the meantime the loyal second must, like dying Hamlet, drag out his painful syllables to tell the truth.

The play ends as it began, among soldiers. Fortinbras enters with his army from Poland along with the messengers from

113

England telling of the deaths of Rosencrantz and Guildenstern. The outside world marches in on the Danish court to witness its rottenness laid bare. And so we are left with Fortinbras, Hamlet's other shadow. Soldierly, resolute, son of another dead king, his self-appointed task has been a kind of revenge for his father's death. Like Hamlet and like Laertes he too threatened Claudius. But his revenge was unjust, his purposes easily turned awry until now. Happening by total chance at this moment to enter the Danish power vacuum he lays his claim to the vacant throne even before he hears that dying Hamlet has cast his vote for him to do just that. How coolly he declares that chance ("fortune", in both senses, not destiny) is acting to his advantage.

> With sorrow I embrace my fortune.
> I have some rights of memory in this kingdom,
> Which now to claim my vantage doth invite me.

(370—72)

The throne lies in his way, and he will fall into it. Like the other Hotspur figure Laertes he has studied the case for revenge only casually, antithesis of Hamlet, and at the last, unhampered by Laertes' plotting or Hamlet's judgement, he carries off the prize.

The play's last irony comes aptly from the mouth of such a man. His only criteria the honours of military action, he orders for young Hamlet a military cortege. Hamlet is "*like* a soldier". And indeed was "*likely*, had he been put on" to have been kingly too. Patronising, uncomprehending, Fortinbras praises Hamlet for his potential not his accomplishment. Even as the source of Claudian evil lies dead in the public view the need for Horatio to voice Hamlet's truth shows in the new king. We are back in the world of old Hamlet, with the sole addition of young Hamlet's story.

NOTES

Studies of *Hamlet* are legion, and studies of studies of *Hamlet* are multiplying. Stanley Wells, *Shakespeare: Select Bibliographical Guides* (London 1973) has a chapter on *Hamlet* studies by John Jump. Patrick Murray's *The Shakespearian Scene* (London 1969) is a survey of modern Shakespearean criticism and critical approaches which includes several references to *Hamlet* criticism. Morris Weitz's *'Hamlet' and the Philosophy of Literary Criticism* (London 1965) discusses twentieth century approaches in Part I and evaluates them in Part II.

Shakespeare Survey 9 (1956) and *Stratford upon Avon Studies* 5 (1963) were both devoted exclusively to *Hamlet*. John Jump's *'Hamlet': a Casebook* and David Bevington's book in the *Twentieth Century Interpretations* series collect together many of the important essays on the play.

Critics have served the play much better than editors. Dover Wilson's edition in the New Cambridge series suffers from editorial interference in its text and especially its stage directions. The New Arden edition has been on its way since the early 1950s and the New Penguin since the late 1960s but neither has yet arrived. The Riverside edition, the latest collected edition of Shakespeare's works, is hugely expensive, and the New Swan edition has careless misprints and rather inadequate notes.

In the absence of any good edition, I have used the most readily available text, the New Swan, for its line numbering and for most of the quotations. The readily available collected edition of Peter Alexander, the Collins text, is printed in double columns and therefore varies widely in its line numbering from other texts in all scenes which have any quantity of prose. Users of the New Swan edition might wish to record the following errata:

I.ii.s.d. Hamlet enters at the end of the procession.

II.ii.555 and III.iii.76 *villian* should read *villain*.

IV.v.14-15 are spoken by the Queen, not Horatio.

V.ii.30-37 are spoken by Hamlet, not Horatio.

IV.v.38 should read *Which bewept to the grave did not go*.

V.ii.150 *german* should read *germane*.

V.ii.357 *his bloody question* should read *this bloody question*.

G I Duthie's critical study of the "Bad" Quarto was

published in 1941, not 1841.

Chapter 1: Organisation and Structure

1. Edmund Malone, the eighteenth-century Shakespearean scholar, records these details, but the evidence on which he based his statement has been lost.

2. There is yet a further irony in this speech, if we give any credibility to the tradition that Shakespeare himself played the part of the ghost at the original Globe.

3. George Buchanan, *De Jure Regni apud Scotos*, trans. F. Arrowood, Austin, Texas 1949, p. 12.

4. *Essayes*, trans. Florio, 1603, p. 480. The direct evidence for Montaigne's influence on Shakespeare was traced by G.C. Taylor, *Shakespeare's Debt to Montaigne* (Cambridge, Mass. 1925), who found many echoes of Florio's English version in most of Shakespeare's later plays. The greatest quantity of echoes are in *Hamlet* and *King Lear*. Doubts have been thrown on the evidence for Shakespeare's direct debt to Florio, but the cumulative indications are very substantial. Verbal echoes, of course, tell us only that Shakespeare read the *Essayes*, not what he thought of them.

5. Ibid., p. 481.

6. Ibid., p. 482.

7. Hardin Craig, "Hamlet's Book", *Huntington Library Bulletin* 5 (1934), pp. 17-37, notes the similarities in *Hamlet* to Cardan's *De Consolatione*, particularly the third soliloquy, and suggests it is indebted directly to Cardan rather than Montaigne. Both writers shared a well-known tradition of meditative philosophy.

8. The names are noted in, for instance, R.F. Gore-Brown, *Lord Bothwell* (London 1937), pp. 409-11, 454.

Chapter 2: The Claudian Globe.

1. G. Wilson Knight, *The Wheel of Fire* (London 1930), pp. 32-41 and 318-20.

Chapter 3: Hamlet's Globe (1): Blood and Judgement.

1. An examination of "reason" and its meanings in
   Hamlet's time is given in Terence Hawkes' *Shakespeare and the Reason* (London 1964). Hawkes dis-
   tinguishes two kinds, the rational faculty which is
   reason at the Claudian level, and a higher, intuitive
   reason which is closer to the angels and which
   Hawkes finds in Hamlet.

2. Coleridge was not the only commentator to see
   something of Hamlet in himself, or of himself in
   Hamlet. Cf. Stephen Potter, *Coleridge and S.T.C.*
   (London 1935), pp. 140-42. Despite or perhaps
   because of this, Coleridge's own summary of
   Hamlet's problem is unparalleled:

   > Shakespeare wished to impress upon us the
   > truth, that action is the chief end of existence
   > — that no faculties of intellect, however bril-
   > liant, can be considered valuable, or indeed
   > otherwise than as misfortunes, if they with-
   > draw us from, or render us repugnant to action,
   > and lead us to think and think of doing, until
   > the time has elapsed when we can do anything
   > effectually. In enforcing this moral truth, Shake-
   > speare has shown the fulness and force of his
   > powers: all that is amiable and excellent in
   > nature is combined in Hamlet, with the excep-
   > tion of one quality. He is a man living in medi-
   > tation, called upon to act by every motive
   > human and divine, but the great object of his
   > life is defeated by continually resolving to do,
   > yet doing nothing but resolve. (T.M. Raysor,
   > *Coleridge's Shakespearean Criticism*, 2 vols,
   > Cambridge 1930, II.154-5).

Chapter 4: Hamlet's Globe (2): Scourge and Minister.

1. Cf. Tigurinus Chelidonius, *The Institution of
   Christian Princes*, trans. James Chillester, 1571. sig.
   Q2v: "*Totilla* King of the *Goathes* being demaun-
   ded wherefore he was so cruell and extreeme
   against the people, answered with a marvellous
   faithe therein, what thinkest thou that I am other
   than the very wrath and scourge of God, sent upon

the earthe as an instrument to chasten the offences and wickednesse of the people? We may evidently therefore knowe by these things that God doth for the most part correct and chasten us by the wicked (who neverthelesse doe not cease to be wicked still, and deserve them selves plagues:) for, according to the word of the Lord and savioure, it is necessary there come slaunder, but cursed be he by whome slaunder shall come."

2. Cf. Emrys Jones, letter in *CQ* III (1961), pp. 72-3.
3. Harry Levin, *The Question of 'Hamlet'* (New York 1959) pp. 72-5, has some illuminating comments on Montaigne, Donne and their resemblances to Hamlet's cast of mind.
4. Cf. L.C. Knights, *An Approach to 'Hamlet'* (London 1960), p. 121.
5. Cf. G. Wilson Knight, *The Wheel of Fire*, op.cit. pp. 32-41.

Chapter 5: The Sequence of Events.
1. Cf. Paul N. Siegel, "Discerning the Ghost in *Hamlet*", *PMLA* LXXVIII (1963), pp. 148-9.
2. An impressive discussion of this point is in Peter Alexander's *Hamlet Father and Son* (Oxford 1951), pp.40-48.
3. Harry Levin, *The Question of 'Hamlet'*, p. 167, presents a diagram of the way in which the alternatives lead round in a circle. Cf. also Vincent F. Petronella, "Hamlet's 'To be or not to be' Soliloquy: Once More unto the Breach", *Studies in Philology* LXXI (1974), pp. 72-88.
4. Cf. for instance Dieter Mehl, *The Elizabethan Dumb-Show* (London 1965), pp. 110-20. See also Dover Wilson, *What Happens in 'Hamlet'* (Cambridge 1935), pp. 144-53, and Clifford Leech, "Studies in *Hamlet* 1901-1955", *Shakespeare Survey* 9 (1956), p. 8.
5. Cf. G. Bullough, *Narrative and Dramatic Sources of Shakespeare* (8 vols, London 1954-75), VII.39.
6. The classic presentation of this view is in Ernest Jones, *Hamlet and Oedipus* (London 1949).